UNDERSTANDING
EQUITY AND TRUSTS

Jeffrey Hackney is a barrister, and Fellow and Tutor in
Law at Wadham College, Oxford.

J.A.G. Griffith is Emeritus Professor of Public Law in
the University of London.

Jeffrey Hackney

UNDERSTANDING
EQUITY AND TRUSTS

Fontana Press

First published in 1987 by Fontana Paperbacks
8 Grafton Street, London W1X 3LA

Copyright © Jeffrey Hackney 1987

Set in 10 point Times

Made and printed in Great Britain by
William Collins Sons & Co. Ltd, Glasgow

Contents

Editor's Preface

This series is directed primarily at two groups of readers: the general reader who wishes to understand what it is that lawyers are talking about, and the law student who is told that he is about to study a subject called tort, or contract, or criminal law, or property, or trusts and equity, or public law. These titles convey little that is clear about the nature of their subjects and the extra-legal meanings that attach to some – such as contract or criminal law – may be misleading.

Each book in this series seeks to explain what the subject is about, what are the special kinds of problems it seeks to solve, and why it has developed as it has. The books are not at all meant to be summaries of their subjects, each of which covers a complicated area of human activity.

The law student will, in his or her course, be expected to read much longer and fuller texts on the subjects, to attend lectures and tutorials. The books in this series seek to provide introductions to be read early in the course or before it begins. It is hoped that these introductions will enable the student to grasp the essentials before coming to grips with the details. So also, the general reader who wishes to pursue the subject more fully will have to read the more detailed texts.

Although these books are intended to be introductions, they are not meant to be simplifications. These are not 'easy' books, however clearly they are written. Understanding law is not an easy matter. This is not, as is often said, primarily because lawyers use words with special meanings. It is because law has to deal with the complications, both personal and commercial, that people become involved in. We are all as busy as ants, more purposeful and sometimes less efficient. Law tries to regularise these complications and so cannot avoid being itself complicated.

The intention of the series will be achieved if the books give the reader a broad perspective and a general understanding of the legal principles on which these different subjects are based.

John Griffith
April 1987

Apologia, or Self-Defence

Students all too often see the law of trusts as a series of disconnected technical problems, which it is their best ambition to conquer one by one, and they are partly right. It is primarily a branch of technical property law, and, like all such law, has a strong planning element. Customers need guidance on how to achieve results, and quite often do not care how to get things done as long as they are told, in minute detail, how to get them right. Since Equity is an ancient jurisdiction, and people have been doing their own thing in it for centuries, the complexity of the law reflects the complexity of the mind of the human animal over the period of its existence: and that is some complexity. In response to these demands, Equity has been woven into a text of fine subtlety.

But students are also partly wrong. The problems are not disconnected. The lawyers have bound each part together with a mixture of social and political and professional values. Lawyers have views like the rest of us on right and wrong; they also have their own professional values about, for example, the nature and limits of property and the way in which contract operates. Law has an intellectual as well as social and political history. These elements combined with a desire to have a working, reliable system, inspiring confidence in its users and encouraging them to come back, have made Equity into a coherent working system supported by these underlying values. The aim of this book is to highlight some of the connections, but more importantly to encourage an evaluative, investigative, and not merely comprehending approach to the study of this part of the law. It is not in competition with any other book. It is designed for students at all levels studying Equity and Trusts, from beginner to graduate student. For the beginner, it has been written to be read twice, perhaps, once before diving into the textbooks, and once again afterwards. It is intended to be an interpretative tool for imposing a system on the mass of materials. The book has fewer than fifty cases, in line with the attempt to keep the wood from the trees. But most importantly, the aim is to stimulate enthusiasm and enjoyment from this seemingly driest of disciplines. The rewards, if reaped, can be immense. The student becomes the hunter, not the hunted. As the sense of participation increases, so does the pleasure; with the pleasure comes added motivation; with motivation, skill and technical mastery; with skill, more pleasure . . .

There is a paradox. On the one hand the law is built around great ideas such as property and contract, and these may be seen in generalised, broad-brush terms. But in the end these ideas receive expression in a working philosophical system like the law, only through detailed application, and only by seeing where the detail fits in can we be sure we truly understand the great themes. Technicality may appear to shield the idea: in fact, it forms a part of it. Natural scientists used to believe that it was only by understanding simple things that they would understand complex things. The opposite is now seen to be true, as it is for law. So the great ideas which dominate Equity thinking will appear sometimes expressed through detailed technicality, in an attempt to discover their true nature. They are all part of the same investigation. The aim is to encourage the student to discover for him or herself the 'arguments and reasons' of the law.

This is not a textbook. Its size dictates that if it were to seek comprehensive coverage, it could be no more (or less) than a set of potted notes. This is simply not its aim. Some subjects have been omitted because by convention they are now taught in other areas where they are better integrated. For the rest, its selective coverage is determined almost entirely by those areas which have most confounded or frightened my students, and it skips over the stuff with which they have felt relatively well at ease. And some subjects are now so much detail and so little principle, constructive trusts, for example, that no attempt is made to set out the catalogue of heads of liability already well documented in the textbooks. Nor is it 'balanced' in the way that textbooks are balanced. It is hard to stimulate involvement by balance, and no one can pretend that there is not enough balance in writing on the law of trusts to keep an armada afloat. In any case, balance is an overtly political value, which, in excess, it is quite unbalanced to practise; too much balance is bad for you.

I once had an old (aged) sculptor friend who showed me a photograph of a rather involved Roman erotic sculpture which had been badly damaged over the centuries and which he had been called upon to restore, and which he had done, so he proudly told me, 'entirely from memory'. I am not sure that is such a good recipe for writing a law book (either), but this book has been, where possible, almost entirely so written in an attempt to keep it readable. If I have to defend myself, lawyer fashion, by citing authority for my lack of citation, I rely on a passage from one of the century's great lawyers and ironists, Karl Llewellyn, who, having written *The Bramble Bush* without many symptoms of what he called 'cititis', nonetheless occasionally worried about it. In a minor attack of self-consciousness on this account he had the answer (page 8): 'The cure is to ask: "Where did Aristotle get his stuff from?" ' No one is more aware of the multiple irony than me. Colleagues and students will hear their own voices on every page.

The law as stated, unless otherwise indicated, is that of the mother country, England and Wales. I have tried and failed to find noun or adjective to express this collective and have too often settled in cowardly fashion for the centrist form. Suggestions on how to solve this will be gratefully received. 'Britain' is not usable as it includes Scotland which has its own legal system and, more importantly for these purposes, its own law of trusts, which has its own intellectual conception and has not relied on the defective judicial structures of the English model.

Part One
EQUITY

1

Laying the Foundations

1. LAW AND EQUITY

THE VERY BEGINNINGS

At the beginning of the nineteenth century, the court structure in England and Wales was in a mess. The population was subject to the jurisdiction of a dual system of superior courts. On the one side were the three 'common law' courts – the Common Pleas, the Queen's Bench and the Exchequer of Pleas – and on the other was the Court of Chancery.

From any managerial viewpoint, this arrangement was ludicrous. The three common law courts had grown up under the authority of the English kings during the Middle Ages. They were known as courts of 'common' law because, according to royal propaganda, that law applied to all subjects and the whole realm, in contrast to the welter of local and specialised jurisdictions which previously prevailed. Only an 'historical' explanation can be offered for why there were three such common law courts with substantially overlapping jurisdictions, and it sets the tone for the rest of this strange story to say that, 'common' or not, they could, and often did, give different answers to the same questions, and that even as late as the nineteenth century there was no reliable method of ironing out those differences. But, and much stranger still, rules based on judgments given in these common law courts, and even the judgments themselves, were in some cases being denied or added to in the Chancery. This was not by way of appeal. The common law judgment was not formally set aside or reversed; the Chancery, while leaving it intact, simply issued an order which was inconsistent with that of the common law judges, and the constitutional position was that this second order prevailed, leaving the common law answer as an overshadowed solution to the problem. These Chancery orders had come to be made by applying a body of doctrine and principles invented initially by the

15

Chancellor, and later by his subordinate the Master of the Rolls (and later still, the Vice-Chancellors). These rules, principles and doctrines of the Court of Chancery, bearing this complex relationship with the doctrines of the common law, were to be known as Equity. This body of law did not however cover the entire area of business which the common law courts had taken as their jurisdiction. It was essentially a 'private law' jurisdiction, dealing with matters raised by private individuals, protecting their private interests. There was no involvement with the common law of crime. The principal focuses of attention were the laws of property and contract, and only incidentally to these was it to develop a law of private wrongs. Equity was not the only jurisdiction exercised in the Chancery, and there were others which their successors exercise today, but it was the one which was to leave the greatest impression on the development of the legal system.

'CONSCIENCE'

Chancery had a reputation as a court administering an individual discretionary justice in contrast to the inflexible monoliths of the common law. Whether this was perceived by all litigants in Chancery (or even at common law) may be doubted, and certainly much of the jurisprudence of the court has been concerned with working out the detailed administrative implications of having taken an earlier moral stance, and many of these decisions, like much administration, have little reference to individuated notions of right and wrong. But the tradition is fundamentally well based and it is impossible to read Equity cases of any period without being aware of it. The explanation for the flavour is, of course, also historical. The early history of the jurisdiction is obscure and in any case quite irrelevant for a modern lawyer. The history which leaves traces begins at the end of the Middle Ages in the early sixteenth century. By that date it can be said that the common law courts had in some areas become inadequate. Outside the law of tort they had shown an insufficient ability to adapt to new claims, and the set forms of writs particularly restricted the development of new issues and defences. There was also dissatisfaction with common law remedies. Despite having taken the inspired decision to enforce rights of property in land by actually delivering it up by force, if need be, to its owner, it enforced other rights, including property in chattels, as well as all contract and tort claims, by a money judgment – the defendant could satisfy the court, if not the plaintiff, by handing over to him a sum of money. Finally, common law pleading had become both overly complex and also a monument to single-mindedness in its stubborn refusal to allow more than one issue to be tried at a time. Reform of these defects by statute was not seen to be an answer, and disappointed parties petitioned the King to get them out of the mess into which his common law courts had put them, and to receive the ordinary justice, the fair and commonsense solution, the equity, which they were otherwise denied.

These petitions came to be heard by the King's greatest officer of state, the Chancellor. By the early sixteenth century, he was giving decisions in his own name and had established a jurisdiction over freehold land. It soon became a trade mark of Chancery thinking to emphasise 'good faith' and to appeal to notions of 'conscience', though there is justification for the view that the intervention was not so much to enforce the good faith solution as to prevent the accrual of benefits arising from bad faith. The avoidance of unconscionability may be the central informing idea. These notions of conscience, which do not figure prominently in the articulation of common law rules, are familiar in the canon law and it is possible that the ecclesiastical background of early Chancellors accounts for this emphasis. Step by step they set about plugging the loopholes left by the common law's shortcomings. Their pleadings were more flexible. They gave orders to parties to do things other than deliver up land or pay sums of money, and so laid the foundations of the modern law of specific performance of contracts and of injunctions. They relieved against accidental hardship and certain kinds of oppressive behaviour, establishing for instance the modern law of protection of the mortgagor. They allowed the creation and transfer of a new kind of intangible property, the right to payment of a debt, developed into the branch of the law known to us by the archaic name of the assignment of *choses in action* ('things protectable only by litigation' – the word 'thing' is always, it would seem, tastefully translated into French or Latin by common lawyers). Most dramatically of all, perhaps, they invented the 'use', later to be reborn as the modern trust. By this device, they would order that property held on a common law title by Y, as his own, should rather be administered by Y only for the benefit of X, the beneficiary of the use. This would often be in consequence of a voluntary (in the sense of 'willing') undertaking by Y, but sometimes it would not. Of greater significance still is that even if there were a voluntary undertaking, it need not have been to X herself, but to a third party, often a relative of X, who had conveyed the property to Y. Uses were not contract. In this way Chancellors supported, supplemented and corrected the common law.

DIFFERENCE AND CONFLICT

The Chancellor's decisions had begun, it seems, as individual decisions solving individual grievances or sometimes simply dilemmas posed by conscientious trustees wanting to know what to do. They were what Benjamin Cardozo called a sequence of 'isolated dooms'. There were 'suits' in the Chancery, not actions, and the Chancellor gave 'decrees' not judgments. The contrast with the regular court system was enhanced by the absence of a jury (which accounted for much of the hostility to Equity in the American colonies, a hostility which was not assuaged by the Chancellor's habit in the home country of cheating in this regard by arranging for a common law jury to give an opinion on some cases) and by the Chancellor's practice of not taking oral evidence. But a combination of repeated circumstance and a desire to treat like cases alike was ultimately to drive the Chancellor into developing a system of rules: equity was to become Equity. The early days of this development were not marked by hostility from the common lawyers, but in the sixteenth century it began to brew. Cardinal Wolsey, one of Henry VIII's powerful Chancellors, had in the 1520s caused much resentment by his encroaching and aggressive behaviour. The so-called 'common' injunctions denying litigants even the right of access to common law courts were also a cause of much friction. Matters came to a head in the early seventeenth century when Coke, then Chief Justice of the King's Bench, challenged the right of the Chancellor, Ellesmere, to override common law results. Coke's appeal to the King in 1616 failed, however, and from that date it has not been questioned that when the rules of Equity and common law conflict, it is the rules of Equity which will prevail.

EQUITY AND THE COMMON LAW IN THE NARROW SENSE

There are now two usages of 'common law': the wider usage, meaning the whole of the royal law, includes Equity; the narrower usage, focusing on the contrast, excludes it. If there was continuing resentment about the divergence after 1616, it did not surface, and relations between the two systems were on the surface amicable, much aided by the diplomatic formulations of equitable rules which hid the substance of what was going on: 'we are not overturning the common law rules; all we are saying is that while Y may own at common law, X owns in Equity', so disguising the fact that X may be happy – Y may not. Equally effectively, decisions were often attributed to the demands of Equity as if it were some creature with a will of its own, some personified virtue, some Marianne, pulling the strings of the judicial marionettes. This mode of speech – 'Equity will not allow . . .' – seems less aggressive than 'I will not allow . . .' to which it must often have been substantially identical. The mode is still occasionally used, and serves to divert the attention of a potentially critical audience from perceiving what might, if otherwise phrased, look like an expression of the individual preference of an individual judge. It can give Chancery law an unnecessary but highly characteristic air of mysticism. What does Lord Brightman really mean when he says, 'There are other circumstances in which equity may infer that the beneficial interest is intended to be held by the grantees as tenants in common. In the opinion of their Lordships, one such case is . . .' (*Malayan Credit v. Jack*, 1986)?

THE SYSTEMATISATION OF EQUITY BY THE CHANCELLORS

In the course of the mid-seventeenth to early nineteenth centuries, Equity was turned into a systematic body of principles as refined, rigorous and ultimately as unyielding as anything produced by the common law. This, however, was a slow process, and it was not complete in the eighteenth century. The letters of Junius, around 1770, could still attack Lord Mansfield, then Chief Justice of the King's Bench, on the ground that he had turned it into a 'court of equity and the judge, instead of consulting strictly the law of the land, refers only to the wisdom of the court and the purity of his conscience'. The final product was the result of the work of a series of professional, legally trained Chancellors. Sir Thomas More (1529–32) might count as the first, but the names of Lords Nottingham (1673–82), Hardwicke (1737–56) and Eldon (1801–6, 1807–27, but hearing cases to 1835) justly figure as amongst the greatest in all stories of this development. To Lord Hardwicke we owe a pair of opposed thoughts of great importance in our understanding of the limits of the Equity jurisdiction. On the one hand he pointed out the self-evident truth that the common law courts were also enforcing obligations which had a moral foundation, especially for our purposes, in their laws of agency and bailments (deliveries of chattels which were often, like their land law equivalent, leases, based on contract). What Equity was doing was conferring rights to enforce conscience-based obligations in situations where the common law would not do so. Equity did not have a monopoly of conscience, and the differences between some of its institutions and those of the common law can be very small, and sometimes seem to be no more than matters of presentation. On the other hand, not every breach of confidence attracted the trust solution, or received sanction in the Chancery. Some such breaches were to be left to the (withering) ecclesiastical jurisdiction or enforced via the forum of the moral disapproval of one's friends and neighbours.

REFORM

But to say that the period 1530–1830 was one of much development is not the same as saying that the system underwent a process of continuous improvement so far as litigants were concerned. In particular the court's attention to detail became obsessive, and its proceedings much delayed. A late eighteenth-century letter-writer complained that it was not easy to escape from the 'amicable gripe of the court of Chancery', and in Lord Eldon's time, Chancery proceedings became a by-word for delay, and his fastidiousness caused much perceived and real injustice. Charles Dickens's *Bleak House* suggests that his immediate successor was no improvement. The reformist mood of the nineteenth century did, however, make its mark on the Chancery. Apart from substantial statutory reform of the court, there were some important innovations from within. The restrictive covenant began its portentous journey from contract to property law, a movement based openly on considerations of fair play. The law of estoppel took a new proprietary turn, and new techniques were devised to cope with the complexities of contemporary financial arrangements. The express private trust developed into a finely tuned instrument for the preservation of wealth. By 1879 a great Chancery judge was proudly observing that Equity was a modern system. Chancery judges were not subscribing to fantastical notions that their law was established from time immemorial, the 'doctrines are progressive, refined, altered and improved; and if we want to know what the rules of Equity are, we must look, of course, rather to the more modern than the more ancient cases'.

2. THE CREATION OF EQUITY'S OWN LAW OF PROPERTY

One consequence of the 'regularisation' of Equity was the creation of a law of property. The Chancellor had originally intervened by imposing personal obligations on particular defendants. So the early trustee of land would be under a personal obligation to administer the property for his beneficiary, but the trustee might still be seen as the owner of the land. The particular novelty of the trust is that the beneficiary need not have been a party to a transaction establishing the trust, yet he is still able to enforce it, and what is more, the person who does set up the transaction finds he has no standing to intervene to see that it is honoured. By the end of this period the beneficiary of the trust is perceived as having an equitable proprietary interest in the asset, not just rights enforceable only against the trustee. He can enforce his rights against total strangers, from whom he can demand the asset. This 'exigibility' – demandability – is one of the characteristics of property. He can also alienate and pass a good equitable title. For some of the beneficiary's protection his trustee will have to use the mechanism of the common law courts, and the beneficiary of the trust may have to invoke the assistance of the Chancellor to drive a reluctant trustee to take the necessary steps. But the trustee is no longer exercising rights. His common law ownership was made up of a set of rights, powers and duties. The Chancellor's intervention has overridden or destroyed the rights, which the trustee can no longer exercise at his own election and for his own benefit, and has converted them into equitable duties, to be performed for the sole benefit of the beneficiary. No principle seems more central to the law of trusts than that the trustee may not derive a profit from the trust. There is today no sensible usage of 'owner' which can apply to the trustee, and every sensible usage which can apply to the beneficiary. The trustee has a legal title and access to common law courts and remedies, but he is a driven vehicle for the superior rights of his beneficiary. He litigates at common law in response to his equitable duties, and not to his common law rights, which have been subordinated. The trustee is now a manager in an institution which is a hybrid between the creation of an agency and the disposition of property.

There are sometimes mistakenly thought to be two features of Equity which prevent us saying that it has produced property rights. The first of these is the rule classically stated in the case of *Pilcher v. Rawlins* in 1872, and the second the motto that Equity acts *in personam*.

(a) The bona fide purchaser of a legal estate for value without notice

This rule states that if a trustee in breach of trust conveys the legal estate in trust property to a bona fide purchaser for value without notice of the trust, that purchaser takes the property free from the beneficiary's interest. The beneficiary has his remedy against the trustee for breach of trust but if the trustee has no assets, the beneficiary loses everything. At all events he has no remedy against the purchaser. How, then, it is asked, can the beneficiary have a proprietary interest, when we know that such interests have to be 'good against all the world', and the bona fide purchaser rule shows that equitable interests are not? The answer is simple, and crucial to our understanding of the nature of equitable interests. In the first place it is important to see what 'good against all the world' does not mean. It is of course impossible in most contexts for an owner to prove that he could succeed against the whole world, and he makes no attempt to do so. The expression is a compendious way of saying that the owner, when he is for example seeking to recover his property from a third party, does not need to base his claim on some prior transaction with that third party or allege that the third party has done him a wrong. The identity of the third party is irrelevant to the case made out by the owner, and he will make out the same proof of his ownership whoever the defendant is. The claim is not like one in contract or tort, where the identity of the defendant is essential to the formulation of the claim. Secondly, it is a characteristic of ownership that an owner may not be able to succeed against a particular defendant because his proprietary interest is defeasible and has been so defeated. There are many examples at common law where owners lose their property in this way, escheat for felony, forfeiture for treason, and wreck being examples. A closer analogy from the common law (though with a quite different theoretical basis) lies in the so-called *market overt* rule. Under this rule, a common law owner of chattels may lose his ownership in them if they are sold in what is known as *market overt*, a market held in a privileged location at certain designated times. A non-owner can pass title to chattels if they are sold in such a designated market at that particular time and in a particular way. No one argues that because common law titles are thus defeasible, there is no ownership of chattels at common law. What is truly odd about the bona fide purchaser rule in Equity and the *market overt* rule at common law is that they stand out from the normal policy of the law, particularly in respect of land. In general, the common law (in the narrow sense) protects vested rights. It is in this sense a capitalist system. Owners do not lose ownership by a mercantile transaction to which they have not consented, and the bona fide purchaser from one who only appeared to have the right to sell, will have to restore the property to the owner. Nor, inside Equity itself, will transactions defeat vested equitable proprietary interests: the bona fide purchaser of an equitable interest from someone who had no right to transfer it will find he has nothing. Only in the third case of a conflict between the beneficiary under a trust and a transferee of a legal estate from the trustee does security of transactions prevail over security of vested proprietary rights. The *Pilcher v. Rawlins* rule cannot therefore sensibly be explained in terms of fair play (unless one is prepared to castigate the 'vested rights' solution as unfair), and indeed it is as hard to see the moral superiority of one side over the other as it is hard to disapprove of a system which comes down clearly and consistently on one side or the other. The only unacceptable position must be the one we inherit, where we sometimes prefer vested rights and at other times transactions, without letting the purchaser of a legal estate know in advance which rule will apply to him. (The bona fide purchaser of a legal estate cannot tell in advance either from the nature of the location or the nature of the subject matter being transferred, whether he is buying from a fraudulent trustee or from someone without a legal title at all who is able to misrepresent himself as legal owner, and thus has no way in advance of knowing whether he will win or lose. The dishonest trustee and the common law crook will look identical to him.) The English explanation of this particular rule comes from constitutional law, from the relationship between common law and Equity, and was clearly seen by at least one of the judges in *Pilcher v. Rawlins*. It is a matter of jurisdiction, not a matter of policy.

THE JURISDICTIONAL BASIS OF THE BONA FIDE PURCHASER RULE

Equity is and always has been an interventionist jurisdiction. It only creates its own interests to be protected when the common law result is unsatisfactory, but it does not operate unless that dissatisfaction exists. Sir Edward Coke is said to have cited a doggerel which he attributed to Sir Thomas More:

> Three things are to be helped in Conscience,
> Fraud, accident and things of confidence.

Perhaps Coke was at the time making a political point about how far the Chancellor could go (*only* three things . . .) and citing the last 'good' Chancellor in support, but the point is nevertheless a good one. Unless you can find a peg on which to hang an attack on the common law's solution, that solution will stand, and Equity will have no jurisdiction to intervene. So when the bona fide purchaser of a legal estate from a trustee for value and without notice is brought into Equity by the beneficiary under the trust, the beneficiary will have to establish that the property was held on trust for him, and call the purchaser to answer. The purchaser's answer seeks to assert that it would not be unconscionable to let him keep the property (even though it might not be unconscionable to take it from him) and he thus seeks to oust the jurisdiction of the court; for this purpose he will himself bear the burden of proof, and a heavy one at that. But if he can prove all the elements of his plea, he will have pulled out all the pegs by establishing that his assertion of his common law title is not unconscionable, that his conscience is not affected; the plaintiff will be nonsuited for lack of jurisdiction in the court; and the purchaser will be able later to defend himself in a common law court, where of course he will win, since that court will not (virtually *ex hypothesi*) recognise the purely equitable title of the beneficiary under the trust, who cannot therefore set up a case. It is thus quite misleading to describe the purchaser as Maitland did, as 'Equity's darling'. Equity shows him no affection at all, he has simply shown himself to belong to that large class of common law owners with whom Equity has nothing to do. He does not win in the Chancery, which should not enter judgment in his favour, since it has no jurisdiction. He wins at common law, which does show him favour, and whose darling he truly is.

CREATION AND DESTRUCTION OF EQUITABLE INTERESTS
The implications are far-reaching. Ownership at common law is a beneficial interest giving its owner economic advantages. The beneficial owner at common law has no equitable interest. The Chancellor has nothing to do with him; the common law gives him all the protection he requires. But if a jurisdiction-generating fact (fraud, acceptance of the role of trustee etc.) occurs, an equitable interest will be created, and the common law title will be stripped of its economic value and cease to be ownership. If a jurisdiction-denying fact then occurs (the bona fide purchaser, for example), the equitable interest is destroyed and the common law title regains its economic value and its quality of ownership. The equitable interest cannot in future bind takers of the legal estate even with notice; it no longer exists (though if the fraudulent trustee himself reacquires the property he will be bound by the trust, since he has a personal obligation, unless he has already settled with his beneficiaries). This capacity of equitable interests to arise and disappear is a key to understanding many of the problems which arise in the setting up and termination of trusts. The solution to this problem is also at the root of what is meant when it is said that Equity is a 'gloss' system. (Maitland right this time.) Equity only operates when the common law result is unacceptable. It does not operate over the whole area, and for the most part leaves the common law to get on with it. It would have been possible in the early nineteenth century to have abolished Equity, and still have left a working (and very unjust or inadequate) common law system. But if the common law had been abolished, there would have been no legal system left at all.

(b) A property system acting *in personam*

The second mistaken objection to Equity's having its law of property is founded on the assertion that Equity acts *in personam*, against the person. It is irritating enough to have the common law expressed in Latin tags, but this one can be seriously misleading. When Roman lawyers say of someone that he has rights of property, of ownership, they say he has rights *in rem*, against a thing itself. This expression implies for them that the identity of any possible defendant is irrelevant to the formulation of the claim, which will be built up in essentially the same way against anyone. When they say of someone that he has rights *in personam*, they generally mean that his rights derive from contract or tort; they may be enforced only against that person who by his conduct has generated them, and the identity of that person is crucial to the formulation of the right. But this is not what is meant when it is said that Equity acts *in personam*. This expression is not used to classify a party's claim or rights, it is expressive only of the ways in which the order of the court will be enforced. Take an example of where a court holds that an asset in the hands of Y is owned by X. That concludes the part of the trial devoted to analysing rights or claims; X may be said to have a right *in rem*. The court must now turn its attention to how to enforce its order. There are three principal choices. It could order Y to hand over the property, and if he failed to do so, send in its own executive officers to seize it and hand it to X. Common law courts took this step for land, sending the sheriff to put out a recalcitrant defendant, and we have therefore called property in land *real* property (enforced against the thing itself – another Latin derivation). Secondly, the court could order Y either to hand over the property to X or pay its value, at Y's election, and if he fails to do so, cause its officers to make raids on Y's property generally and either holding what is taken until Y pays, or selling it and distributing the proceeds to X to the value of the order. This is how the common law originally protected property in chattels; no one was obliged by the court actually to hand over the chattel, property in which was not therefore *real*. Thirdly, the court might simply order Y to be put in jail until he performed, or caused to be performed, the order of the court. This might be described as acting *in personam*, against the person, and this is how the Chancellor enforced his decrees in the early days of his jurisdiction.

26

The *in personam* phrase is not descriptive of X's rights, but simply describes the mode of execution of the court in protecting them – property rights protected by imprisoning contumacious violators. One can protect rights *in rem* by judgments *in personam*.

3. 'TRUSTS'

This is not to say that all persons seeking equitable relief in the nineteenth century were asserting proprietary interests. Some, seeking specific performance of contracts or injunctions to restrain breach of contract or to prevent or remedy the commission of a tort, were openly relying on rights which were not proprietary. Nor was it essential for all beneficiaries in all varieties of trust to assert such a proprietary interest. The essential idea behind the trust seems to have been to secure a result rather than to project forward from some legal premise about property. As the trust became increasingly regulated by the operation of precedent, its use as a planning tool was greatly enhanced and it became institutionalised, that is, its use carried with it a whole package of rules which would be applied to the parties in the absence of clear contrary intention. 'Trust' became a descriptive term with a hard core of content. Parties could thus find themselves bound by rules which they had never contemplated, but which they could, conversely, if they wished, trigger by the use of a few choice words. It is in this usage, that of the express private trust, that we see the most thorough elaboration of results from proprietary first principles. The institutional trust is sometimes contrasted with the remedial trust, where the court imposes a trust, the terms of which may be tailor-made to suit the circumstances of the case and may omit many if not all of the managerial features of the institutional trust. Putting different types of trust clearly into the one category or the other is not an easy matter, particularly since this has not been a terminology beloved of judges, and because some types of trust seem to share characteristics of both. The principal value of such categorization is to alert us to the range of the trust usage.

A recent international conference (Hague, 1984), whose conclusions are due to be implemented, for conflict of law purposes, as the Recognition of Trusts Act 1986, has encapsulated the essential characteristics of the institutional trust. First, the assets constitute a separate fund and are not a part of the trustee's own estate; second, the title to the trust assets stands in the name of the trustee or in the name of another person on behalf of the trustee; third, the trustee has the power and the duty, in respect of which he is accountable, to manage, employ or dispose of the assets in accordance with the terms of the trust and the special duties imposed on him by law. (This convention reminds us that other legal systems have devices which are similar to the trust, which they have developed out of other ideas, primarily contract, since they were not impeded by our primitive court structure.) But even within the range of clearly institutional trusts there is variety. Some, like trusts for charities, have never been imagined to be based on equitable property vested in beneficiaries, but there are others, like discretionary trusts, where that truth has been harder to see. Some judges have been so taken up with the proprietary model of the express private trust that they have tended to undersell, if not to miss, the richness of the trust model. We have now reached the point where assets which are owned by no one may be held on trust for ascertained beneficiaries, who do not have an equitable proprietary interest. This notion of ownerless property which is nonetheless not open to acquisition by taking by a third party – it is not up for grabs – is a remarkable and increasingly prevalent feature of modern Equity, though it has existed as an idea since the days of classical Roman law. One of the greatest errors in creative thinking in trust law is to begin unguardedly, 'This is a trust therefore . . .' and to proceed to attribute to it the characteristics of the express private institutional trust. There are many different kinds of trust, the only common feature of which may be that they involve, or once involved, identifiable property and are subject to a legal regime originating solely in Equity. Perhaps it would better reflect the origin of the jurisdiction to say that there are many different kinds of trustee, ranging from the willing manager to the entrapped villain.

4. THE MAXIMS AND DOCTRINES OF EQUITY

The systematisation of conscience, which had such beneficial effects on the growth of the trust, had also some effects which have not been so obviously beneficial in the long run. Amongst these might be numbered the evolution of the so-called 'Maxims' and 'Doctrines' of Equity. The former are a collection of mottoes in which aspects of conscience became pickled and to a degree trivialised. So, He who comes to Equity must come with Clean Hands; Equity is Equality; Equity will not assist a Volunteer; Equity looks to the Substance, not to the Form; Equity Looks on that as Done which Ought to be Done; and so on. Apart from a vigorous life in law examinations at the pen of weaker candidates, most of the maxims do not today greatly figure in judicial language, and their principal harm is, by their banality, to reduce manifestations of justice to the level of simple chatter, and thereby to devalue the underlying conscience.

The same cannot be said of the Doctrines of Election, Satisfaction, Ademption and Performance, Conversion and Reconversion. These doctrines bear the stamp of a social world which has long gone and were devised to provide simple fixed (and therefore, in a sense, efficient) answers to problems, usually posed by testators, to which there was no obviously simple moral solution. In the modern context, lacking most of their original justification, their inflexibility looks like arbitrariness and they have justly been said to exist principally as traps for the unwary. A recent prominent example of a combination of maxim and doctrine, operating quite unsuitably in a modern context, has been in the area of the ownership of the family home. Where such homes are in shared ownership, they are all thought, as the result of an Act of legislative imprescience in 1925, to be held on a 'trust for sale'. This device imposes a legal obligation on the trustees in whom the legal title is vested, usually in these cases the cohabiting co-owners themselves, to sell the house forthwith, but gives them, subject to certain conditions, the power to postpone sale. (Not an easy notion to explain to new homebuyers.) When the property is sold, the co-owners take the purchase money. The doctrine of Conversion provides, with some sense in situations where the trustees and co-owners are different people, that instead of the interests of the co-owners being turned into money at some unpredictable moment, over which only the trustees may have control, the interests of the co-owners shall from the beginning be deemed to be interests in money. There is some evidence that the doctrine was applied originally somewhat selectively and not at all times for all purposes. But, if Equity Looks on that as Done which Ought to be Done, arguably we should treat the trustees as having sold the house at once, and so treat the interests of the co-owners as interests in money from the beginning, and for all purposes. This view seems to have prevailed in some quarters. This interesting debate rapidly loses its metaphysical flavour when a co-owner finds that by statute, interests in land are better protected against third parties than are interests in money, and having acted in reliance on the land mechanisms, is told by a judge that the interest is one in money, and so not protected. A combination of an awkward statute and an unconfident handling of this ancient Chancery law has caused anxiety, expense and, as some think, simple injustice. It is hard to believe that if the doctrine of Conversion had not existed, we would, at least in this context, have needed to invent it.

2

Reform by Statute

During the late Middle Ages a number of piecemeal attempts were made to regulate the use, which for all present purposes might be described as the trust under an earlier name. This was primarily aimed at preventing uses from being employed for various kinds of sharp practice. Unfortunately for the medieval landowner, however, one of his principal reasons for wanting a use, namely to make a will of land (which was impossible at common law), also brought him into conflict with the royal revenue interest, since much taxation was gathered when land passed to the heir on death. Henry VIII, in an attempt to put a stop to this once and for all, in 1536 enacted the Statute of Uses. Put simply, this statute, by a parliamentary conveyance, as it were, took the legal estate in the use away from the 'trustee' and vested it in the beneficiary. This was known as 'executing' the use. It was probably intended to put an end to uses, and to this portion of Equity jurisdiction, for all practical purposes. The right to make wills of land at common law was, as the result of rebellion, granted shortly afterwards by statute, and the King protected his revenue interests in other ways. But this meant there would now be no royal objection to uses when they began to reappear as trusts, with the legal and equitable title again separated. For reasons for which at present we can only make intelligent conjecture, however, the conveyancing of trusts began with the creation of an executed use, to vest the legal estate in the trustee. This practice was rendered meaningless in England and Wales only when the statute was repealed in 1925, though it persists in some common law jurisdictions in North America. It is not impossible that we have not seen the last of this statute, but it is enough to know that it is there, and to know that big books exist to solve problems which might arise. The rest is legal history.

One hundred and fifty years later, in 1677, with the trust in full flow, and during the Chancellorship of Lord Nottingham, Parliament

31

intervened to reform the excessively informal law governing the creation of certain trusts, most notably wills and trusts of land, and the assignment of certain equitable interests. This enactment, the monumental Statute of Frauds, has been superseded in England most notably by the Wills Act of 1837 and by the Law of Property Act of 1925. Two more centuries passed before the next significant reform, the Chancery Amendment Act (Lord Cairns's Act) of 1858. This statute gave the Chancery, for the first time, the power to emulate the common law by making awards of damages instead of, or in addition to, an injunction or specific performance. The statute has, reasonably enough, been a cause of some puzzlement to later judges since Equity could only give an injunction where (the common law remedy of) damages were inadequate, and though the jurisdiction to make such orders continues, the scope for debate was much reduced by the cataclysmic events of 1873–5 which scrapped the dual system in England and Wales and set up a unified judicature.

A UNITARY JUDICATURE

As early as the late eighteenth century many states of the USA had given the Equity jurisdiction to their common law judges. Others had tried the dual system, but some, like New York in 1820, had gone for single judicature. Georgia and Texas had actually abolished the distinction between law and Equity. The states of Australia and the provinces of Canada had in substance adopted the dual system, though often the same judge would wear the two different hats, and as at Westminster, some had begun to make minor dents in the line between the two jurisdictions. The Westminster Parliament by the Judicature Acts of 1873–5 now sought to rub it out. The idea was to have law and Equity administered in the one set of courts with each judge having both jurisdictions. This was to be true both for trial judges and for the appellate system. All superior trial judges were to be members of one court, though with separate divisions to which business was assigned. The most important consequence, perhaps, of this latter provision was that it in no way affected the growth or stability of the specialist bars which had attached themselves to the ancient courts. Specialisation, both in advocacy and, because of the way judges continued to be selected from the bar, amongst the judiciary, was maintained (though at appeal court level, 'non-specialist' judges may be hearing appeals from the other 'side'). The idea was not to attempt a fusion of common law concepts with those of Equity, but to have them both administered in the same room by the same judge: defences to equitable claims were not to be applied to common law claims, and those with equitable rights only were not to acquire the advantages of common law enforcement. This thinking is not unlike that behind the 1858 Act, that is to save time and money for litigants, as well as removing a judicature system which was as disgracefully structured as it was venerable. The problem of how the judge was to react if he found himself at the same time administering common law and conflicting equitable principles was solved by enacting the 1616 settlement: when the rules of Equity and law conflict, those of Equity are to prevail. Litigants were generally free to choose to which Division to take their business, subject to certain limitations imposed by the statute and by subsequent orders. This legislation set up the modern Chancery Division in London and was shortly followed by similar legislation in Canada and Australia. New South Wales stood out as the sole custodian of tradition in the Commonwealth, only abolishing the dual system in 1972. Some separate Equity jurisdiction still exists in the USA, but its duality is not rigorously applied.

STATUTORY SIMPLIFICATION OF STRUCTURE AND NOTICE

There were further statutory provisions which had a major impact on Equity principally relating to settlements of land, but by convention they are allocated to books on land law. Also to be found there, but having a wider relevance in Equity, were the reforms of the *Pilcher v. Rawlins* doctrine, mainly in the twentieth century. Some jurisdictions have completely restructured their land law conveyancing, using the language of equitable and legal interests, but subordinating their protection entirely to the statute's own scheme, with varying degrees of extremity. The Westminster Land Registration Act of 1925 is a moderate example of such a statute. Other statutes such as the Law of Property Act and the Settled Land Act 1925, from the same legislature, have intervened at a less drastic level. First of all, the number of legal estates were dramatically reduced. Equitable interests were then divided into two principal groups. Some, mainly family interests, were made overreachable, that is, conveyance by the trustee to a third party results, if done properly, in the interests of the beneficiaries under the trust being converted into the proceeds of sale. The purchaser takes free of the interests of the beneficiaries, who must now look to the money in the hands of the trustees. Notice is irrelevant. The second group, mainly commercial interests, were still subjected to the *Pilcher v. Rawlins* idea, but the matter of notice was now (subject to a reservation affecting persons in possession) to be settled exclusively by looking at the state of a public register, rather than by looking at the conduct of the purchaser. So in theory a purchaser who knows of such an interest, but finds it is not registered, takes free of it.

It is no surprise that judges have not always been willing to give these provisions their literal effect, both here and in the seemingly more rigorous Land Registration Act: not all such purchasers are immediately attractive, and some of them have found themselves bound by the use of the device of the 'constructive trust', a device not contemplated by the legislation. This is reminiscent of judicial treatment of the Statute of Frauds 1677, where judges invented the theory that they would not let a statute designed to prevent fraud be used as an instrument of fraud, and so ignored its seemingly mandatory provisions. Perhaps the most startling finding to emerge with respect to the Law of Property Act scheme, however, is that a small group of equitable interests seem to have slipped through the net and are neither overreachable nor registrable. They are still subject to the old bona fide purchaser rule, as are most equitable interests in personalty (chattels etc.). This rule cannot now be based on jurisdiction, for the judge will have both jurisdictions, but no one seems to have taken any notice of the fact that the bona fide purchaser rule has in effect been demoted by the Judicature Acts, and that judges are now in theory free to opt for security of vested rights in all cases, the constitutional restraints which previously bound them having been withdrawn. The statutory reforms of notice have, of course, reduced much of the urgency.

3

The Extent of the Contemporary Jurisdiction

Not all common law jurisdictions now administer exactly the same business as Chancery law. In England and Wales, the business presently administered in the Chancery Division of the High Court is set out in the Supreme Court Act 1981, as follows:

(a) the sale, exchange or partition of land, or the raising of charges on land;

(b) the redemption or foreclosure of mortgages;

(c) the execution of trusts;

(d) the administration of the estates of deceased persons;

(e) bankruptcy;

(f) the dissolution of partnerships or the taking of partnerships or other accounts;

(g) the rectification, setting aside or cancellation of deeds or other instruments in writing;

(h) probate business, other than non-contentious or common form business;

(i) patents, trade marks, registered designs or copyright;

(j) the appointment of the guardian of a minor's estate,

and all other causes and matters involving the High Court's jurisdiction under the enactments relating to companies.

This curious hotchpot of business is what remains of the multifarious jurisdiction which the Chancellor had either assumed or been given over his long history. If we describe as Equity only that part of the jurisdiction where the Chancellor was reacting to the common law, all of this is not Equity. Of the list, (d) and (h), which make up the law of succession, were subtracted from the old ecclesiastical and common law courts, and are not Equity in this sense. Bankruptcy was a jurisdiction conferred by statute on the Chancellor personally, and is also not Equity, though it borrows heavily from equitable techniques. The technical law in (f) and (i) and that relating to companies is also not Equity; it was assigned to the Chancery because it had the apparatus in its accounting procedures, which it had evolved for the administration of deceased estates, to handle the complex financial matters which this business brings. It also borrows heavily from Equity. Until 1970 the Division also had a wardship jurisdiction, exercising the royal prerogative in which the monarch assumed the role of guardian of the kingdom. In addition there is some assigned business, notably appeals from the Charity Commissioners, and business under the Variation of Trusts Act 1958. A separate jurisdiction over testamentary gifts to charity, which does not look like Equity either, does not clearly fit under any one head: while (c) and (d) are the obvious places, neither seems to fit exactly. The old remedy jurisdiction, including, principally, specific performance of contracts and injunctions, is not in this list because since 1875 these remedies have been available in any Division of the High Court.

THE SINGLE JUDICATURE AND AN EFFECT: WALSH V. LONSDALE

Although it was intended that the rules of law and Equity should be jointly administered only, and not fused into a single-rule system, the parallel administration has from time to time caused difficulties, one of the most famous of which grows from the decision in *Walsh v. Lonsdale* (1882), arising from the remedy of Specific Performance. This is a contractual remedy in Equity in which the court compels a defendant to carry out his contract, and it applies to cases where the court considers that the common law remedy of damages is inadequate. This remedy, being limited to contract, has not seen the same developmental growth as its companion remedy, the injunction, which may command or forbid behaviour, which applies to any kind of legal right, and which has been extended to a variety of circumstances to prevent the stealing of marches (interlocutory), and to prevent threatened harm (*quia timet*: 'because he fears'). Specific performance has somewhat withered in the commercial law, where damages are most often an adequate remedy, but it has retained a thriving life in the land law because the Chancery judges followed the opinion of the common lawyers (when enforcing proprietary, not contractual rights) that land was special, and accordingly in this contractual situation held that damages would be inadequate.

The Extent of the Contemporary Jurisdiction

At common law, a vendor would remain owner of the land even after he had agreed to sell it, only losing his proprietary rights when he finally made a conveyance, and in the meantime the purchaser was limited to the remedy of damages for breach of contract. In Equity, the court would order the vendor to specifically perform his contract by conveying the land. By applying its maxim, however, that Equity looked on that as done which ought to have been done, and pretending that it had given the remedy when the contract was made, Equity managed to blur the distinction between owning and being owed. It treated the purchaser as if he were already owner and converted the vendor into a kind of trustee, today known as a constructive trustee because the trust is said to be constructed (not construed) by the court. But they were not wholehearted about it, and the vendor was allowed to retain some benefits from the land pending actual conveyance, a sort of hybrid between trust and contract: the vendor is half owner, half trustee. These trusts bind third party assignees of the land, subject to the normal rules about bona fide purchasers etc. Though the original purchaser takes the trust benefits, he has no trust obligations and he is bound only in contract. Such contracts became known as Estate Contracts, and they were incorporated into the statutory schemes for notice of equitable interests mentioned above. Such trusts would also arise on the sale of a limited proprietary interest in land, such as a lease or an easement. If the purchaser were actually awarded specific performance, he would no longer be a beneficiary under a trust, he would take his legal proprietary interest and would use the common law remedies appropriate to a grantee of such an interest. But until that moment the parties were confined to their simple contract remedies at common law or their complex contract/trust remedies in Equity, under the pretending game. Finally, if the subject matter of the transaction was a legal lease, once it existed, third party purchasers from either party might be bound to perform special duties which the original parties had by covenant undertaken and which attached themselves to the 'estate' created by the lease: in the case of contractual arrangements, third parties could take the benefits of such arrangements (as is the case for all contracts) but could not be bound to perform the duties.

The question which arose after 1875 was whether, since the same judge exercised both jurisdictions, he would, pending conveyance, play the pretending game when wearing his common law hat. If he would, then the parties could rely on their common law proprietary remedies, even though specific performance had not yet been granted and the conveyance not yet made. The court in *Walsh v. Lonsdale* held that a common law remedy could be applied even though a common law proprietary interest had not yet been created, and a new maxim was spawned: 'An agreement for a lease is as good as a lease.' But just as their Chancery predecessors had had an ambivalent attitude to the constructive trust, the new dual jurisdiction judges have not been willing to face up to the implications of this decision or to develop the old law. What we need to know is whether an agreement for a lease is not merely as good as a lease, but whether it actually is an equitable lease, creating an estate to which covenants might be attached, in which case burdens as well as benefits of covenants would be transmissible to assignees. The problem is partly caused, in the case of leases, by the continuing bilateral relationship of the parties after the conveyance, in a way that is not the case for an outright grant of the land. If the constructive trust notion is to produce a true equitable lease, it will have to attach the trust obligations to both sides of the bargain. At present the courts have shrunk not only from treating the parties as if they had a legal lease for all purposes, but also from the conclusion that in Equity there is a lease with proprietary characteristics capable of holding contractual terms which will bind third parties, just as a legal lease does. Orthodoxy says that the constructive trust doctrine is bedded in contract, affects only the parties to the deal so far as covenants are concerned, and has not created a fully fledged equitable proprietary interest capable of binding assignees of the 'lessee'; unorthodoxy says it has created such an interest and lays the development at the feet of the 'fusion of law and Equity'. Unorthodoxy here has much to be said for it from a pragmatic point of view, in a world where sealed common law leases are not universal practice. But if Chancery judges wish to turn the agreement for a lease into a fully fledged property interest, an equitable lease, they can do so by developing the pre-1873 constructive trust into an equitable proprietary interest, and they will not need the *Walsh v. Lonsdale* doctrine to do so. The creation of new equitable estates, and the question of whether those estates will attract common law attributes, are two different matters. Extensions to affect third parties by deeming into existence legal interests, such as 'legal' leases, attracting 'legal' consequences, where none have been expressly created will be a more difficult, and more chaotic result; true 'fusion' indeed.

Further complexity has been caused, however, by attempts to apply the 'treating as done' doctrine not just to cases where the contract is for the sale of a property interest in land, but also to any contract where permission is given to be on land, the so-called law of licences to enter land. These attempts have received one major rebuff, being described in *National Provincial Bank v. Ainsworth* (1965) as examples of the 'contract fallacy' – if a contract is specifically enforceable or its breach restrainable by injunction as between A and B, then it will bind third parties who take from A or B – a classical confusion of categories. Although the restrictive covenant began its momentous journey in Equity from contract to property on the back of the same 'fallacy', a journey which it continues to make, there seems no judicial appetite for repeating the trip with a new passenger.

EQUITY AND SOCIAL CHANGE IN THE LAND LAW
Elsewhere in the land law, the judges are facing a dilemma which must be common to all developed legal systems; do we keep to well advertised rules, known to the profession and relied on by them, and, in the interests of system-efficiency and the overall reduction of cost, send away litigants with whom we have considerable personal sympathy, but who have not complied with the rules; or do we never send away deserving litigants without redress, and let the system worry about how the new exception is to fit in, given that all judgments are precedents? This debate, which is of course so much easier to conduct in the classroom, where you don't have to see the parties, than in the courtroom, becomes particularly difficult in times of rapid social change, where arrangements made in one period and leading to a clear result in that period, come to be seen to be socially unjust in another. Such times also raise important questions about the legislative functions of the courts in relation to Parliaments. Courts can at best conduct only piecemeal reform, creating in the process much uncertainty, which means anxiety and expense, while legislatures, properly so called, can enact schemes of reform covering a whole area. Is it better for a judge who wants reform to try to bring it about fractionally or to hand down a judgment which applies the old law in all its newly perceived harshness? The former may

persuade Parliament that it can sit back and let the courts do the job; the latter may sting it into action. This has been the problem in England and Wales in the last two decades over ownership of the family home. Where previously it seems to have been socially acceptable, if not desirable, for a male spouse to have full ownership, and the law certainly gave effect to such a result, it has now become accepted at all levels that some kind of shared interest in the family (formerly matrimonial) home is often what is wanted. Judges have reacted differently to this challenge and there has sometimes been a marked divergence in England between those with a common law and those with a Chancery background, the latter generally putting more emphasis on the planning elements.

The battle has been fought in a number of ways. Sometimes the issue has been seen as one about the creation of co-ownership in land, as judges try to lose the commercial origins of the doctrines, sometimes as an estoppel problem, sometimes simply as a matter of how to construe land registration statutes, and sometimes as a matter of constructive trusts. Some judicial dissatisfaction has been expressed with this patchwork, and it plainly needs some high-level sorting out. What all these cases have in common is a desire to be fair to individuals when existing rules would send them empty and unfairly away. This is classically the origin of the jurisdiction, but Equity is now on grounds of fairness having to modify its own creations.

EQUITABLE OBLIGATIONS ON THE CLEAN OF CONSCIENCE

In a quite opposite development some judges have also been developing the constructive trust to prevent unconscionable conduct by spreading its net so wide as to catch not only those whom they believe to have been behaving badly, but also those who, while innocent of any personal bad intent, are able so to present themselves because they have been taking an unduly carefree approach to wrongdoers with whom they have come into association. This is a familiar problem in Equity. The concept of notice in the bona fide purchaser doctrine had to be extended to catch not only those who had noticed, but also those who had not because they went around with their eyes closed. In a related matter, Equity has also rejected the notion of the 'sleeping trustee' – the trustee who had failed to spot a breach by his fellows because he had absented himself from the business of the trust. By now making liable as constructive trustees those who should have been aware of wrongdoing going on around them and in which they innocently assist, and so in a sense developing an objective conscience liability, the courts are raising the standards of commercial behaviour and generating in effect a liability in negligence. (More on this below, at page 163.)

STATUTORY CONSCIENCE

A final area worthy of note in general Equity is its partial replacement by statute in one of its earliest areas of intervention, the law of mortgages. Chancery judges have for long been most tender, if not too tender, in their protection of the mortgagor, by creating a number of devices, some of them none too clearly based on conscience, for setting aside advantageous bargains made by mortgagees. They had, however, more or less, and rather shamefully in contrast, left other borrowers to fend for themselves, and in the matter of unconscionable terms, Parliament has now intervened in the Consumer Credit Act 1974 to regulate a wide range of credit bargains, including mortgages, in a way which some think the Chancery judges should long ago have done. The Unfair Contract Terms Act 1977 is another reflection of a job the judges failed to do being taken over by Parliament.

RANGE OF APPLICATION OF THE MODERN
INSTITUTIONAL TRUST

But perhaps the most remarkable of all changes is that which has taken place in the range of function to which the trust is now being put, only a part of which is detectable from a reading of the law reports, because the basic ideas of the trust have proved remarkably resilient in adapting to new needs without requiring judicial creativity. Trusts have long been used for a range of purposes, honest and dishonest, and they have taken a number of shapes. They arise both when parties knowingly and voluntarily create them and when they do not. When we came across the trust earlier, we focused on the paradigm three party trust, set up by consenting parties, which is reflected in the language. First there is a benefactor who, if alive, we call the settlor, who transfers property, the subject matter of the trust, by way of gift to a trustee, who is to hold it for the benefit of the beneficiaries, or objects, of the trust. These latter would usually be identifiable individuals, often the family of the settlor, though the object could be a charitable purpose. The trustees are conceived of as family friends and hence have no entitlement, unless they have made a special arrangement, to any remuneration. Such trusts continue to be made, but it is probably safe to say, without undertaking a counting exercise, that the majority of trusts of any substantial value no longer fit the social picture so depicted.

To begin with, the increased complexity of trust instruments, trust law and the economic and fiscal background have caused the amateur trustee to be joined by trustees who are professionals and who undertake the work only for proper reward. Some large trusts only have such trustees. And the trust itself may be set up as a commercial venture, entirely without element of gift. Sometimes, as in trusts which manage pension funds, the subject matter of the trust is in whole or in part provided by the beneficiary. Sometimes the settlor may settle his own property, or property which he undertakes to procure from a third party, but may do so in return for a valuable consideration provided by the beneficiary: commercial investment arrangements can use this mechanism, and trusts to pay one's creditors are another example with a different flavour. Again, the trustee himself may provide the value of the settlor's transfer, and this might be a feature of family arrangement trusts made on the dissolution of a marriage. But not only may trusts not be gratuitous, they may not involve three distinct parties. In the pension fund case, the settlor and beneficiary may be the same person, and it may be that a beneficiary in such a case is also one of the pension fund trustees. And a person may declare himself to be a trustee of his own property, so combining trustee and settlor, and may include himself in the list of beneficiaries of his trust. It is thought to be possible for a settlor who has provided all the subject matter of the trust to give his trustees power to declare new trusts, so making them in a sense settlors of another's settlement, and in some areas of the profession, it is even believed that a testator can use the same device, so allowing his trustees in effect to make his will for him. Thus it will be important to keep separate the three possible hats. The only limit to this mad hatter's tea party would appear to be that I cannot declare myself trustee of my own property on trust absolutely for myself, since, to return to the reasoning in *Pilcher v. Rawlins*, there is no reason for Equity to intervene and assume jurisdiction, as the common law handles this problem entirely satisfactorily. There is no equitable interest.

The range of use of the trust today defies listing, and approaches in its versatility the range of application of the contract mechanism. We can, however, identify some main purposes. The first of these is the management function. Trusts can be used to permit beneficiaries to enjoy the fruits of property without the necessity of themselves managing it, either because they are incompetent by reason of age or mental disability, too superior to be bothered with such stuff or, like most of us, not having the time or skill to devote to complex matters. This managerial function can be very protective. The so-called Protective trust and its even more extreme American twin, the Spendthrift trust, go so far as to prevent the assets falling into the hands of the creditors of profligate bankrupt beneficiaries. The Discretionary trust will in some circumstances effect a similar result, and this has the added advantage for some settlors that they can allow the trustees to choose their beneficiaries for them from amongst a designated range. In the co-ownership context, the device of the trust for sale constitutes an operating system with a stable legal title, behind which the beneficiaries can program their wishes without the need for constant 'heavy' conveyancing of the legal estate. Indeed, where there are multiple beneficiaries/owners outside the land law, the device of the trust seems to be the only practical way to give effect to their multiple interests, and this is particularly true when some of the beneficiaries are not yet born or ascertained, but their 'interest' needs present protection.

A second function of the trust, which may overlap the first, is to secure financial benefits. Primarily this is a reference to public finance. The sophistication and flexibility of the trust have made it an ideal tool for tax planners, and the new Inheritance Tax in the United Kingdom puts a high premium on a mastery of the technical minutiae of the law of trusts. Social security law is another parameter, and settlors wishing to make provision for individuals in distress – through disability, for example – will have to be aware that such provision may reduce state benefits, and much ingenuity is devoted to preventing this from happening. Both of these motives can produce trusts of extraordinary complexity, which, since the motive is hardly likely to be expressed, can appear puzzling to the beginner. Indeed, for these purposes no distinction is too fine, no shade too subtle, and much of the most complex law of trusts has grown up in response to a stimulus from the law of public finance. The other financial benefit is to avoid the consequences of someone else's bankruptcy. Property held by a bankrupt on trust for another does not go into the pool to be shared out amongst the general creditors; it is returned to its owner. The trick therefore is to persuade a court to identify property held by the bankrupt as being on trust for you, and so to that extent defeat the general creditors. The Tracing remedy was one way of achieving this, and more recently in the commercial context there have appeared reservation of title clauses which seek to achieve the same result. Happily in the commercial context, where both parties are trading, judges have not been as tender to the tracer, and hostile to the general creditor, as they have been in the past when the tracing was sought on behalf of a family trust.

Finally, trusts may be used to achieve purposes. The clearest example is the law of charities, but it may be possible to achieve purposes outside this predominantly altruistic area. This is a characteristic which trusts share with contract and it will be discussed fully in the next part of the book.

A FUTURE FOR EQUITY?

It must be top of every student's mind to ask why we do not abolish the distinction between law and Equity, whatever that might mean. Equitable defences would be available perhaps to common law rights and people without Clean Hands could get specific performance? The bona fide purchaser rule would go? No separate rules for dispositions of equitable interests? Presumably the law of trusts would in substance remain, since this is not the abolition of Equity, but it would have to be differently expressed.

This must at one time, long ago, have been an option, and of course in America it has been done. But the risk is all on the customer. It would be impossible to guarantee that rule-fusion would not create real uncertainty and therefore litigation for many years and, indeed, it is virtually certain that it would. The customer would thus bear the risk for the lawyers' tidying up. The same arguments were persuasively raised against a proposal in the 1960s to abolish tenure in the land law: it was undoubtedly an anachronism, but abolishing it might just have unsettled the occasional title; viewed against that harm, reform would have been mere indulgence. Already in the sixteenth century it could be said that the Statute of Uses had caused such uncertainty of title that the nation's inheritances had been tossed as upon a sea. If this was true then, we must invent a doctrine of the over-ripe time to resist reform now. In the land law there has been some movement in this direction. The Land Registration Act 1925 uses the language and concepts of equitable title, but subordinates them to its statutory scheme, and as that statute comes to cover the whole land, some subordination of the importance of separating the two systems will have taken place.

Part Two
TRUSTS

A. TRUSTS INTENDED TO BE CREATED

Trusts have three 'parties': the party from whom the property derives, the party who is to hold it, and the party (or purpose, as we shall see) for whose benefit it is to be held. Subject to what we saw earlier about people wearing more than one hat at once, the intention of the third party in this list is not regarded as relevant to the formation of a trust. In this main section we are dealing with trusts which are formed when both the first and second parties (settlor and trustee) have an intention to create a trust. We are looking for what might be called 'express intention', however manifested. It is the express intention of the first party, however, which is paramount. The same rules will apply when the second party, who has not been consulted by the first, declines to act, provided that he simply wishes to bow out and not to claim the property beneficially for himself. Similarly if he is unable to act. 'Equity will not allow a trust to fail for want of a trustee': the court will arrange a replacement. We are not here considering cases where the court supplies an intention as a way of giving what it regards as the proper effect to a dealing, or where it simply imposes a trust to achieve a just result. Nor are we dealing with situations where the second party seeks to divert to himself a trust benefit intended for another. There may, however, be one small exception: the trustee of a fully secret trust has told the settlor that he will be a trustee, but he does not mean it, and by relying on a statutory defence he can, unless Equity intervenes, get away with keeping the property for himself. He is not easy to classify. He is treated here with other intended trustees, but he has affinities with constructive trustees who are treated later, and will be picked up again.

Our settlor, in the simple cases now under consideration, has to *settle property* on *trust* for approved beneficial *objects*. The notions of property and its settlement are closely interdependent and will resist all efforts to keep them apart for purposes of exposition.

4

Intention to Create a Trust

MORAL OR LEGAL RELATIONSHIP?

Debates about intention centre around two questions. Our starting point is a dealing with property (we are not trying to distinguish intentions to create trusts from intentions, say, to get married). Did our settlor intend to impose a moral obligation only on the trustee, or was he seeking to create a legal relationship? If the latter, what kind of a relationship? The first question is in theory the easy one, even if in practice it can give rise to difficult interpretative enquiries. Equity's conscience is an artificial notion which is not coterminous with morality. Though not all judges see it clearly all the time, the mere fact that I undertake a moral obligation is not enough to make me legally bound. The moral forum, with its sanction of disapproval of neighbours, continues to exist. But it is not enough merely that I intend legal relations, if the legal relationship proposed is not one which the law recognizes. My intention is a necessary, but not a sufficient, condition. The enquiry is to see whether parties intended to place themselves within the ambit of an existing legal relationship or a new one which the courts should recognize. If there is a legal relationship, the second question arises. Is it for example a bailment, in which case the rules of common law were deemed by Equity to be largely satisfactory, with the bailor/deliverer remaining in control; or is it a contract with ownership passing to the transferee, or a species of contractual agency with the transferor again remaining in control; or is it a power of appointment, or a trust? Infuriatingly, people will not confine their transactions to a single legal category, and in any one transaction there may be a combination of bailment and contract or a combination of contract with trust. The reservation of title cases mentioned earlier are a good modern example of the last, turning on whether the settlor/beneficiary/vendor can claim not to have given dominion over the property to the transferee/purchaser.

TRUSTS AND CONTRACTS

Contracts to create trusts are commonplace. But can we merge contract and trust in one transaction? The answer may have serious consequences for fourth parties. Suppose a company is short of liquid money and is anxious that this should not be known. A quite laudable aim in many cases: there must be employees, shareholders and creditors who have been grateful that a company concealed a bad patch and prevented a loss of confidence in the marketplace which might have resulted in premature dissolution. But what if a company wishes to make an arrangement with a new creditor to borrow money in these circumstances in order to maintain the show, and wishes to give that creditor not only its usual profit if the ruse works, but also priority over everyone else if it fails? The company borrows money from an investment house in order to pay a dividend due on its shares. The arrangement is secret and so the adverse publicity which would have attended some sort of mortgage arrangement of the company's assets is avoided. Employees and other creditors are not put on guard. The aim is to use the money to pay the dividend and thereafter for the company to repay the investment house. And if the dividend cannot for some reason be paid, the parties agree that the investment house shall have its money back. It is the choice of contract or trust as a means of arranging for this return of the investment house's advance that has the wide-ranging social consequences. The money is paid over. Plainly, while it may be said to be given to the company, it is not advanced by way of gift. The company now becomes bankrupt and the dividend may not by law be paid. The general creditors and employees claim that the money was transferred to the company by way of loan, so that the company owned it and could impress it with a trust for the payment of its dividend creditors. That trust now being impossible, the company should hold the money as its own property, to be shared out amongst all the creditors as the law provides. The investment house argues that the arrangement by which the money was to come back to them if the primary purpose, the payment of the dividend, failed, was a trust, not a contract. This secondary trust would mean that the money held by the company would be on trust for the investment house and would not go into the general bankruptcy pool to be shared amongst all creditors, but would return entirely to the house. Property held on trust for another is immune from bankruptcy distribution. The other creditors, who may in the meantime have continued to increase their indebtedness to the company, lose out. If the investment house is right, it has impressive consequences for the nature of some trusts. The company would be trustee, and the investment house the settlor, of the primary and secondary trusts. The house is also beneficiary of the second. Performance of the first trust by the company will result in the creation of a debt by the trustee company to the investment house. If the company spends the money on something other than dividends, it will be in breach of trust and liable for the amount. In other words, both due performance and breach by the trustee will have identical consequences, a unique and difficult notion. In economic reality the settlor of both trusts is the company, which underwrites them. In which case, when the show stops, the money held by the company belongs to it and is owed to its general creditors. But in such a case the investment house won in the House of Lords, and on some rather sketchy evidence: *Barclays Bank v. Quistclose Investments* (1970). This is what is meant when it is said that loan and trust can exist together. It is not analytically defended in the Lords in terms of the nature of trust and contract, and a new creature is invented to protect from risk of failure a secret commercial venture undertaken for profit by two parties at the ultimate expense of general creditors, to whom English courts have too often shown such insensitivity. Disputes about classification are not about how many angels can dance on the head of a pin.

TRUSTS AND 'BARE' POWERS OF APPOINTMENT

In both of these arrangements, property will be vested in a manager, for distribution to or amongst 'objects', who will usually be people or classes of people, but may be purposes. The settlor's intention tells us which he intended. First of all, trusts are mandatory, they impose duties on a trustee to distribute the property in a specified manner; the simplest example of this is the 'fixed' trust where the trustee has a duty to distribute, in amounts fixed by the instrument, to individuals or amongst a class of objects. Powers are discretionary and give discretions to their managers (referred to as donees of the power) whether or not to make a distribution of the property: if they do, they are usually allowed to select objects from amongst a class and to fix the amounts they give. In the simplest case here, the 'bare' power, the donee can with impunity at once forget about the whole thing and do nothing at all, and when the time limit for exercising the power expires, the property will pass in default of action, which in the absence of express provision will usually be back to the transferor, but in any event, it will be at his direction. Secondly, with a trust, the trustee will be managing property which is either owned by an object or is ownerless (charities, and discretionary trusts, for example), and one of the clues to discerning the settlor's intention is to ask whether he has purported to vest the property in the beneficiaries, or at least to divest himself. With a power, the property remains vested in the transferor (called the donor of the power), and the donee has power to give or 'appoint' to B property belonging to A. In some situations courts are prepared to treat donees of powers as if they were owners if they have unlimited discretion as to whom to appoint the property: but that 'as if' is important – if you give me your car I can give it to anyone I like, but it is not right to describe me as having a power of appointment over it, and to do so is to make an unusual confusion of substance and form. If you have transferred ownership to me, I cannot have a power of appointment, and if I have a power of appointment over property, I do not own it. It is this 'appointment' which gives this particular group of powers their name, and which distinguishes them from, in particular, the administrative powers of trustees.

POWERS OF APPOINTMENT GIVEN TO TRUSTEES
'AS SUCH' AND DISCRETIONARY TRUSTS OR 'TRUST
POWERS'

Successive generations of draftsmen have, however, and particularly of late, muddied this simple picture. In the first place they have chosen to combine elements of both trusts and powers of appointment in the same arrangement. Bare powers, the simple institution with no duties, are now hardly found at all. Instead settlors set up trusts and vest their trustees with ancillary powers of appointment. If these powers are vested in the trustees 'as such' – that is, by virtue of their office and will devolve on their successors when they cease to be trustees – then they are fiduciary powers, held for the benefit of others. In this case the law imposes on them a number of duties. So in addition to their power to appoint and their power to select, these trustee-donees have a duty to consider whether or not to exercise the power and to make a survey of the range of possible objects and to consider the appropriateness of any particular appointment. A more extreme mix is the modern discretionary trust, or trust power. Here, in a trust for a class of objects, the trustees have a duty to distribute, which is the basic trust underlay, but they are also given by the settlor a power to select, from amongst the class, which of the objects shall receive the property. In this case they also acquire the same duties which attach to fiduciary powers, though it seems they will be in more severe form. In the simplest case of both powers and discretionary trusts, the trustees will be told they can both select which of the objects shall receive, and decide how much each recipient takes. But settlors are not tied to this, and might for instance give discretion as to the amount but not the persons, or vice versa. In no case may a trustee/donee distribute to a non-object.

The complexity of modern settlements until recently carried with it a hazard. It is often difficult to tell whether a settlor has intended a power or a trust. This is particularly the case when he adds a power of accumulation to the mix. Imagine a trust where trustees have a duty to distribute income annually amongst Class A, and to hold the capital on trust for Class B, which will take it at the end of a time period. If he has a power of accumulation, the trustee can defeat his duty to make a distribution of the income by exercising a power to turn the income into capital. The exercise of this power constitutes a delayed form of appointment to Class B. Trustee inertia in respect of accumulation favours Class A. On the other hand a settlor might give his trustees only a fiduciary power exercisable out of income amongst Class A, but say that if the power is not exercised, then Class B is to get the undistributed income. Trustee inertia, in respect of the power to appoint, favours Class B. Distinguishing between these two creatures, as a matter of construction of the instrument from amongst the often convoluted instructions given by the settlor, can be no easy matter. Quite apart from sorting out what happened if the trustees did nothing, the sting was that the law imposed quite different requirements for initial validity for trusts and powers with respect to certainty of objects, and so the validity of the whole instrument could turn on whether there was a power or a trust with accumulation provision. Recent developments have reduced but not eliminated this problem, which we shall shortly reach.

5

Property as Subject Matter

Any subject matter which qualifies as property will suffice as the subject matter of a trust. So tangible or intangible moveables and immoveables (legal or equitable), choses in action (such as the right to payment of a debt), shares in companies, and even the present right to income, can be impressed with a trust. Subject matter of a commercial value to which the courts have not granted the imprimatur of property, like news, will not do. Nor will property which does not presently exist, or is not yet in the hands of the settlor (future property), suffice, since the establishment of the trust is a property transaction, and there must be property in existence at the moment of creation. It is a matter for debate whether the interest of the beneficiary of a discretionary trust may itself be the subject matter of a fresh trust. We have also followed a long European tradition and required that property must have defined limits if it is to be accepted as the subject matter of a trust. This partly follows instinct – if you claim something is yours you must state clearly what it is, and not expect the court to help you discover it – and partly cultural resistance to the acceptance in property law of what contract lawyers know as the *quantum meruit* developments, where the court would help you discover what you were owed, by asking what you deserved. A further good reason in trust law for sticking with tradition is that the trustee needs to know exactly what property is entrusted to his care.

A seeming exception to this requirement is the notion of the fund. Shares, land, money or any other form of investment may be bundled together as a single investment unit and placed in trust, and the trustees may have power to change the investments. It may then be the case that the fund may change in composition and value from day to day, and that we will not be able to predict with certainty what the investments will amount to at the end of any period. Indeed, a deferred capital beneficiary may here, as always, find that the trust property is worthless by the time the interest vests in enjoyment. But the property will have been identified at the beginning of the period, and by ordinary accounting procedures the contents of the fund can be traced throughout its life, as new investments represent older ones. The trustee's sale of such investments in the ordinary course of his administration of the trust will pass a good title even to a purchaser with notice, since the sale is not in breach of trust, and the *Pilcher v. Rawlins* doctrine applies only to dispositions in breach. So a trustee can defeat a beneficiary's right to any particular investment by exercising his fund management powers, though the beneficiary will be entitled to the proceeds. And to the extent that he incurs costs in the administration, or has a power to pay himself for work done, he may absolutely defeat beneficial interests in the value of the assets. What matters, however, in fund thinking is that the fund is certain at its commencement, even though the beneficiaries' interests are defeasible.

LOGIC, NOT LIFE? THE CASE OF UNADMINISTERED RESIDUE

There is one area where a restricted view of the need for certainty of subject matter has put the law aside from ordinary lay perceptions. It has been held in an important Australian appeal, *Commissioner for Stamp Duties (Qd) v. Livingston* (1965), that people entitled to residue under a will ('residue' being what is left after administration costs and specific gifts have been accounted for) have no proprietary interest in the residue while the deceased's estate is still in the course of being administered (though it is accepted that administration constitutes 'in a sense' a trust, of which they are beneficiaries). It is not altogether clear whether the case decides that the executor has the beneficial interest, or whether it decides that no one has it. The former is not only repugnant to common sense and ordinary use of words – 'beneficial' comes from 'benefit', which is one thing personal representatives never get in any shape or form today (though once they did – which may be how the rule derives), but also produces difficulties if he makes dispositions which are not authorised by his administrative powers and duties. Plainly the easiest way in which beneficiaries can recover property from unauthorised alienees is to say that they own it, since the alienee may have done no wrong. The explanation for the decision in this case seemed to be that there was no certain subject matter over which the trust net could be thrown, since no one knew at the beginning of the administration how much, if anything, would be left at its end for residuary beneficiaries. If this is logically carried through, it covers all testamentary gifts since we cannot know on death the relationship between the deceased's debts and the gifts made in the will, and so whether anyone will receive anything.

The court could have looked at the matter differently and applied fund-type thinking, regarding the estate as the fund and using a notion of defeasibility to take account of the residuary legatee's disappointment, as the administrators lawfully defeat his property by paying off the deceased's debts and their own expenses. The debate is not just a classroom topic. Let us say Spouse 1 dies, leaving a few small gifts here and there and the residue to surviving Spouse 2. It rapidly becomes obvious to Spouse 2 that the debts are going to be a small fraction of the estate and that the family home, formerly owned entirely by Spouse 1, will be in the residue. Spouse 2 now makes a will leaving the house to X and then dies before the estate of Spouse 1 has been administered. X takes nothing because at the date of Spouse 2's death, Spouse 2 did not own the house and could not therefore dispose of it. All Spouse 2 had was a right to have Spouse 1's estate properly administered, and that has not been disposed of. Courts will strive to pretend that it is this latter right that Spouse 2 in fact devised, but it will not always be possible, and the law is not well serving the customers in this respect. It appears to be an example of analytical thinking getting in the way of the reasonable expectations of non-lawyers, and all the more unfortunate since there does appear to be a lawyer's answer to the problem.

6

Objects

1. INDIVIDUALS

Objects of a trust, everyone agrees, must be certain, except in the case of charitable trusts, where for the public good, if the objects are not certainly defined, the court will make a 'scheme' to cure the uncertainty. But it is one thing to agree that objects must be certain, and quite another to agree what certainty is. So set out, the subject has an air of irredeemable dryness about it, but it is not value-free and raises issues of judicial administration with which judges have recently had to grapple. We have also been able to watch as they have attempted to make sense of what their superiors say, and still produce justice in the case before them. The exercise has been a good topic in Equity for observing judicial technique and how the law is made.

When dealing with a trustee's power – say, to determine whether a beneficiary is satisfying a residence requirement – courts have taken a somewhat homespun approach, asking whether the requirement was certain enough in its 'core', and not worrying too much about 'penumbral' uncertainty, even though such a decision effectively shifted entitlement (*Re Coxen*, 1948). But when the issue of object certainty has been before them, they have in recent years developed something of a fondness for tests, and the symposium has become inextricably entwined with that of certainty of the objects of a power of appointment.

CLASSIFICATION OF OBJECTS OF POWERS OF APPOINTMENT AND TRUSTS

Individual objects of a trust or power will qualify either because they are specifically identified or because they are part of a group identified by reference to a description, that is, they form part of a class. In the first case it seems we have to know who the beneficiary is,

57

presumably settled on an intuitive approach. In the latter case, we have for convenience divided classes into three kinds. The first is a general' class, which has no excluded parties, seemingly the whole world. Second, there is a 'special' class, with a limited description which objects must satisfy, such as 'employees of a company', or 'children'. Third, there is a middle category, called variously 'hybrid' or 'intermediate', where the objects are a general class less a special class, like 'all the world except my children', or minus identified named individuals, like 'all the world except myself and my wife'. These three classifications of object can be combined with the classifications of the settlor's intentions as to how the benefits should be bestowed. So, we have powers of appointment for general, special and hybrid/intermediate groups, known shortly as general, special and hybrid or intermediate powers. But as a matter of analysis, at least, we can combine these three classifications of objects with all four varieties of dispositive arrangement we met in the section on subject matter – bare and fiduciary powers, and discretionary and fixed trusts, giving us a starting position of twelve different arrangements.

INTERESTS TO BE CONSIDERED IN FORMULATING A TEST

Since courts are prepared to strike down dispositions in favour of classes of objects on the grounds that the objects are too uncertain, they have signalled that the settlor's views, or those of the trustees, are not conclusive on the question of validity. Here, as in the matter of intention and subject matter, a number of interests are at stake, some of them conflicting. Settlors have their own conflicting interests. In general terms they want a relaxed test, as that will result in a greater chance of their dispositions being held valid. But they do not want too relaxed a test, as they do not want trustees to be able to play fast and loose with their intentions. Objects or potential objects (those within range of the settlor's benevolent intentions) have a similar dilemma: wide tests will increase their chances of qualifying, but once qualified they will not want a test so wide that they cannot easily calculate their chances of success if they wish to challenge a particular appointment by a trustee on the grounds that the appointee was a non-object. The trustee's selfish interest is in a tightly drawn test. He must administer the trust properly, according to its terms. A conscientious trustee will want a test that allows him to do that with a minimum of doubt, and of course he faces the unique difficulty that if he pays to the wrong objects either on a valid or invalid trust or power, he will have to make good the deficit, and though courts have power to excuse him, they do not always do so. A trustee in sympathy with the aims of the settlor will be likely to want a test which is less strict, and so he too will settle for a compromise. The public interest is in having a test which does not result in continuous litigation. Litigation is a particular evil in this part of the law, which is overwhelmingly dominated by planning considerations. The ideal is that the law should be capable of formulation in such a way that legal advisers can produce instruments that are free of legal defect and which can operate entirely outside the court. Until court lists are much reduced, courts have better things to do than involve themselves in the luxury of avoidable disputes about certainty of objects, which both hold up other business and cost money to beneficiaries. It is an abuse of judicial power for a judge to say that he is happy to have a relaxed test in the interests of enhancing settlors' wishes, and that if anyone has any problem with operating it, all they have to do is go along to see him. The public also presumably has some input in the kind of freedom of disposition which they are happy for settlors to have, and this may differ from the freedom they might themselves wish, were they not considering the public interest.

The tests

(a) THE 'COMPLETE LIST' TEST

While it is generally unwise to explain what judicial thinking is 'really' about, there have been enough clues in the last two decades of judicial debate on the tests of certainty of objects for class gifts for it to be clear that the issues listed above have been only slightly in the background as the tussle over precedent has raged, with the settlor's interest tending to win the battle. The story begins in 1948 when, in the *Broadway Cottages* case, the Court of Appeal held that a discretionary trust was only valid if the trustees could draw up a complete list of all the objects. 'Could draw up' seems to have been a commonsense notion, turning on resources and time. Trustees must be given a class which is sufficiently clearly defined, and there must be some reasonable prospect of drawing up the list, though they were told it would not affect initial validity if they did not know with certainty whether, for example, Uncle Bill, last seen on the boat for Australia, was alive or dead. So it seems to have been assumed that a discretionary trust for a general class, which had a perfectly good definition (or was 'conceptually clear', as the newer phrase goes) and for which in theory you could always draw up a complete list, was always void because in practice there was no prospect of being able to draw up such a list. Also void, presumably for the same reason, were the vast majority of hybrid trusts (though these two types of gift may well be like the philosopher's unicorn – conceived but never perceived). Some trusts for special classes were good, and some bad, either because one could not define the class or because, although there was a definition, one could not sensibly be said to be able to draw up the list. The better view at present is that that test was also intended to apply to fixed trusts for classes, though that cannot have been part of the *Broadway ratio* since the case involved a discretionary trust. This complete list test is the strictest which has been discussed, but is a good one for trustees: they know at once how big the class is, and they can know who all the members are and so can perform their duties of consideration and survey efficiently and conscientiously. They can handle the trust without recourse to the court, and are unlikely to make the mistake of distributing to a non-object. The test is a good one for objects within the list for the same reason, but not so good for those settlors whose settlements it struck down, nor, for the same reason, for potential objects whom it deprived of benefactions.

(b) 'IS OR IS NOT'

At the same time there was thought to be a more relaxed rule for powers – can you with certainty say whether any given individual is or is not a member of the class? There was no need to draw up a complete list. All you needed was a good enough definition and a prospect of being able to say of anyone you looked at that they did or did not fall within the definition. If you could not say so, either because the definition was too vague – 'old friends' – or presumably because it was in a practical sense impossible – 'people who have given up their seats for me on the train' – then the gift failed. So all general powers were good; hybrid powers were good if the excluded class was well defined (though there seems to be no test of certainty for the non-objects in the excluded class); and some special powers were good, and some bad. This test is satisfactory for trustees, though they were less well able to perform their consideration and survey duties, and better for settlors and objects and potential objects because it was certain enough to permit challenge while permitting an extended range of valid settlements.

This test was confirmed for powers by the House of Lords in the case of *Re Gulbenkian* in 1968, and substantial support put the way of the 'complete list' test for trusts. But opposition to the *Broadway Cottages* test for trusts was not stilled; if anything, it was stimulated. Some felt that too many discretionary trusts were failing under that test, which was therefore too severe. Company welfare trusts were singled out as examples. What was worse, trusts were failing which would have been good had they been drafted as powers, and telling the two apart was, as we saw earlier, in some cases a difficult matter which cannot have left anyone feeling confident in the result. The courts had also decided that they would not validate an invalid trust by recharacterising it as a power.

The challenge was accepted in 1970 in a trusts case, *Re Baden*, when the House of Lords with a crucially different change of personnel, overturned *Broadway Cottages* in its application to discretionary trusts and applied the powers test to them. The substantial similarity between discretionary trusts and fiduciary powers was set out and emphasised, and the perhaps inevitable commercial result reached. There was now a common test of certainty, it seemed, for discretionary trusts and powers, and the need to undertake embarrassing construction summonses, eliminated. Discretionary trusts were now valid even where we did not know all the beneficiaries, and the court would not be bound to execute the trust, if the trustees failed, by dividing up the fund in equal shares, but would make a scheme of distribution. In a sense, the way had been paved for this reform by the decision in *Gartside v. IRC* (1968) which was the first of a series of cases to establish that objects of a discretionary trust do not have any equitable proprietary interest in the subject matter. It was thus less important for them, as co-owners, to be listed, nor could they individually demand something as of right if the trustees defaulted. Fixed trusts for classes appear to have escaped the *Baden* amendment and are certainly as outside the *ratio* of this case as they were of the earlier one. The 'complete list' test still applies to them. The result was widely welcomed. A substantial concession had been made to settlors and it was to be expected that the law would settle down. But it did not happen, for two reasons which have all the appearance of accident and have left the law in a most uncertain state.

TINKERING WITH THE TEST IN THE COURT OF APPEAL:
RE BADEN, NO. 2

In the first place, the House of Lords in *Re Baden* were not asked to pass on the validity of the instrument before them. They were asked only whether it was a trust or a power, and if it was a trust, what the test for validity was. It was agreed to remit the instrument back to the Chancery Division to see if the trusts established by the deed were valid. The deed contained a discretionary trust in favour of a class which included 'relatives' of a company's employees. It seemed obvious what would happen: the court would construe relative to mean 'close blood relation' or 'next of kin', or some such, which was obviously what Mr Baden had in mind, and validate the trust. It could all have been over in half a day. But it did not turn out like that. Instead of validating the trust after construing it, counsel decided he could do so without having to construe the document. He argued that since the ordinary meaning of the word 'related' meant 'tracing legitimate descent from a common ancestor', that therefore 'relative' meant someone tracing such a descent without limit of time. Whether it is possible to switch meaning from adjective to paradigm noun in this simple fashion may be doubted, as it may whether this is a remotely ordinary meaning to give to 'relative'. If 'relative' did have this meaning and the 'is or is not' test were applied, the trust would fail, since plainly it could not be said of the great majority of the population that they were *not* related to an employee of the company. This appalling result could be avoided, however, counsel argued, if we realised that despite the courts' having formulated the rule in its 'is or is not' form for the best part of a generation, it was open to the court to snip off the 'or is not' bit, and ask if we could say of any given individual that he was within the class of relatives. If so, the trust was valid. Trustees could adopt a relatively passive role and wait for claimants to appear; if they could show they were related in this sense, and therefore in the class, the trustees should consider them. 'Relative' was a 'conceptually certain' word and that was enough: mere 'evidential' difficulties would not defeat the court or, therefore, the gift. A majority of the Court of Appeal decided to boldly go down this road and promptly modified the test laid down barely a year before by the House of Lords, by removing the 'or is not'.

This case is hard to commend as a matter of judicial technique. The law is thrown into uncertainty for the cost of a construction summons. Trusts with vague characteristics ('people who have given up their seats for me on the train') are unnecessarily validated on the certainty test, to await being struck down under some other and equally vague residuary power of the court, such as public policy, capriciousness or perhaps administrative unworkability, which we shall next come to. Not the least of the authority problems created for the new test is that it is plain that if all you need do, under the new test, is to say of any given person that he is a member of the class, it is enough if you can say it of one; such a test had been expressly disapproved for all class gifts in the House of Lords in *Gulbenkian*. Megaw LJ appears to have been sensitive to this, and so invented another wholly new test that you had to be able to say of a 'substantial number' that they were within the class.

This case has left the law in a curious state. The authority position is unclear; three tests for certainty for trusts compete. The law will now permit trusts with conceptually certain classes even though seemingly the trustees may have more often to venture to court to have the evidential difficulties solved, though it must be said that no such ventures have been reported. It is equally hard to see how trustees in their new passive role can claim in good faith to be administering their trust faithfully according to its terms. One solution for a first instance judge might be (and has been) to construe the kind of gift we are looking at not as a class gift, but as a series of individual gifts subject to a condition precedent (proving membership of the class), where the truncated 'is' rule has long been good law. This in itself will complicate the law and introduce the old fear of construction exercises. In any event, it seems it will only work where trustees have a pool of fungibles they can share out. If the benefaction is of a collection of different items, this device will not sort out competing claims to the same item since the trustees do not have the discretion to do so. No doubt the good sense of the overwhelming majority of settlors and the common sense of trustees is preventing an undesirable social result. Presumably the *Baden* trustees have construed their instrument and settled on some sensible meaning which they are now applying, or else are sensibly exercising their discretion to exclude distant relatives on the basis that they were never intended to benefit. But the law in this area is designed to cater for the unusual without recourse to court, and it has to be asked how many of the policy considerations in choosing a certainty test were considered, and are now satisfied. It must also be asked on what ground, legal or social, the Court of Appeal might be justified in departing from House of Lords authority.

(c) A QUASI-CERTAINTY TEST? 'ADMINISTRATIVE UNWORKABILITY'

The second development is no less curious and is perhaps fortuitous. Undoubtedly a key to understanding some of the more difficult passages in Lord Wilberforce's speech in *Baden* is to see that he was trying to minimise the differences between his own views and the opposite ones so recently expressed by Lord Upjohn in *Gulbenkian*. In the course of his defence of the rule in *Broadway Cottages*, Lord Upjohn stated that a trust could fail, quite apart from ambiguity of definition (presumably to keep his head up, he would now have to talk about 'conceptual uncertainty'), because for some 'curious' settlements 'it may be quite impossible to construct even with all the available evidence, anything like a class capable of definition'. This was a difficult passage and it was far from clear what general guidance was intended. Lord Wilberforce, without referring to its *Broadway Cottages* context, imported part of it into the new 'is or is not test', where its function is even less obvious. What is worse, in this new version, two new elements were included: 'There may be a third case where the meaning of the words used is clear but the definition of beneficiaries is so hopelessly wide as not to form "anything like a class" so that the trust is administratively unworkable or in Lord Eldon's words one that cannot be executed.' The two new elements are thus 'width' and 'administrative unworkability'. The questions abound and have caused much expense to subsequent litigants. Does this provision come into effect, after the operation of the certainty test, to strike down all 'general' and 'hybrid' discretionary trusts, so maintaining continuity with *Broadway Cottages*? (They had been void under that test because we could not draw up a complete list.) If so, since donees of a fiduciary power have duties which are different only in degree rather than in principle from those of discretionary trustees, as *Baden* established, are general and hybrid powers also void? Is it an objection, even to a special class, that it is very wide? Lord Wilberforce gave as an example of a trust which might fail 'all the residents of Greater London'. Would this fail as a power too, and if not, why not? Which of their duties is it that the trustees cannot perform in the one, that they might be able to perform in the other? These questions have exercised the minds of first instance judges ever since, and they have struggled to make sense of the passage under consideration while giving effect to a bias in favour of freedom of disposition. On present evidence it would appear that this is an important bias, despite dangerous talk of striking down gifts as 'capricious'.

There is one final conundrum. It is a truism to say that discretionary trusts are governed by the *Baden* rule, whatever it now is. But settlors will not confine themselves to simple models. What are the limits of discretionary trusts? Does a transfer to trustees on trust 'to distribute £1000 each to such members of class A as they shall in their absolute discretion think fit' raise the same administrative problems as a transfer to trustees on trust 'to distribute whatever in their absolute discretion they shall think fit to each and every member of class A'? Is the latter a discretionary trust governed by *Broadway Cottages*?

2. PURPOSES

If the objects of a trust are not simply individuals, they may be purposes. Purpose trusts raise a new set of social, political and economic problems quite apart from the enhanced judicial techniques called for to handle them. These are trusts in which the trustees are directed to perform, or cause to be performed, a purpose; they cannot simply pay over money to others without ensuring what they will use it for. The uses to which the assets are to be put are an essential part of the trust. In a public purpose trust, a charitable trust, the purpose is conceived to be for the benefit of the community, and private individuals receive a benefit only incidentally to the fulfilment of the purpose. So poor people may receive cash from trustees of a trust to relieve poverty, but the trustee cannot make further payments to them once the donees have moved out of poverty.

Such trusts are enforced not by private individuals but by the Crown's Attorney-General, as guardian of the nation, under the royal prerogative (probably the same prerogative that linked this jurisdiction with the Chancellor in the first place).

(a) Charitable purposes

The courts have decided that these trusts must have three characteristics: they must confer a benefit; that benefit must be conferred on the public or a sufficient section of it; and that benefit must be of a sort that the law regards as charitable. This last point is decided by looking at what previous judges have accepted as charitable and by analogising from those decisions, which themselves derive from a statutory origin based on the social perception of charity of the late sixteenth-century (sic) Tudor state. Charity is probably the weakest intellectual product of the Chancery lawyers. Although it is said that benefit has to be proved, that proof is required only after a number of major cultural assumptions have been made with respect to some purposes. So, for instance, it cannot be challenged that religion or education are beneficial, and when courts wish not to confer the benefits of charitable status on trusts they do not approve of, they have been forced into unedifying debates about whether certain sects are religious or not, and even odder debates about what education is. If we were to set this system up anew today we would surely not want lawyers to be arbiters of religious schism. The notion of public is also highly politicised. Private medicine and education are both charitable and may benefit the people who use the services, but it is well known that a substantial section of the community believes these services to operate to the detriment of those who have the same needs but cannot afford to use them. Yet the courts either will not discuss the issue of the wider public, or when they do, the debate – witness the treatment given to private medicine in *Re Resch* (1969) – can be intellectually disgraceful. And the 'analogy' provision means that adjusting the law to current needs is doubly difficult, as judges find the dead hand of past social value constricting the way ahead. It has been said that the law of charity consists almost entirely of issues of fact masquerading as issues of law, and this analogy exercise is a powerful contributor to this characteristic. This has been particularly noticeable since 1960, when all attempts by living persons to establish charities were sent first to the Charity Commission, whose place on the hierarchy of precedent, were they a court or exercising a judicial function, would put them at County Court level, unable to touch even High Court judgments. Since an appeal from the Commissioners is said to cost a five-figure sum, it is not surprising that it rarely happens. The major fault is not with the Commissioners or (even) with the judges, but with the system which allows them to retain this jurisdiction which the latter long ago stole. Neither has the sort of research departments needed to make empirical (as opposed to cultural) findings of 'public benefit', and while the adversarial system may suit the resolution of disputes between parties, it is not well suited to what in effect it is doing here, effecting social and fiscal engineering. As a result, a series of questions framed in empirical form are getting anything but empirical answers. Charities have no real claim to being described as Equity, and it must be an arguable proposition that Chancery judges ought not to be handling the substantive content, as distinct from the mechanism of the trust itself – a distinction they are well able to draw in their control of private trusts. For the debate is not about theory, it is perhaps the most socially controversial matter which they handle. The charity label is an accolade and apart from its value in loosening the purses of donors, brings two substantial advantages, apart from the immunity from certainty law mentioned above.

CHARITY AND TAXATION

First, charities attract a measure of fiscal relief which in some jurisdictions is very substantial. This inducement is responsible for a good deal of distortion in the law. It can be hard to fathom why commercial companies fight so hard, and resort to such deviousness to establish charitable trusts for the education of the children of their employees, until we see that the income of the trust may be tax-exempted, and that payment to the children may not be the taxable income of the parent. Companies can thus achieve a substantial measure of tax-free benefit for their employees, quite apart from the obvious, and virtually undetectable abuse that trustees can pay, not to deserving children, but to the children of deserving parents. And as in any area where tax immunity is bestowed, some very technical lines appear between very similar objects. It is a

Understanding Equity and Trusts

reasonable inference that judicial views on who should, and who should not, get tax relief have in recent years turned charities into a most bizarre branch of the law, and the legal usage of the word is increasingly parting from its ordinary lay usage.

CHARITY AND PERPETUITIES: THE VESTING RULE

Secondly, charities have a limited immunity from the 'perpetuities' law. This law is designed to prevent people from retaining control over their wealth for too long a period into the future, and at common law that period was a lifetime (there were curious rules about whose lifetime counted) and twenty-one years thereafter. Statutes throughout the common law world have now provided their own period and their own ways of choosing lives. The 'rule' against perpetuities is in fact probably at least two rules. First, in its original common law form, it prevents gifts *taking effect* at too remote a date in the future by striking down gifts which could by any chance 'vest in interest' outside the perpetuity period. At common law one had, almost without exception, to look at possible, not actual events, and so one could, by the exercise of imagination, say from the moment the instrument took effect which interests would, and which would not, satisfy the rule. Modern statutes have amended the rule to the extent that we now may look at actual events, a kinder regime to 'beneficiaries', but one which can hold up knowledge of the validity of dispositions for three generations. Vesting in interest might generally be said to occur when no contingency remains to stand in the way of entitlement and might be earlier than when enjoyment actually begins. Charities have only a limited immunity from this rule. A gift to a charity, following after a gift to an individual, which vests/might vest (depending on jurisdiction) outside the period, will fail. But a gift to charity B, following after a gift to charity A, which vests/might vest outside the period, will be good: the gift is regarded as having been vested in charity all along.

CHARITY AND PERPETUITIES: THE RULE AGAINST
PERPETUAL DURATION

The second rule is the rule against perpetual duration. This rule would prevent a purpose trust from *lasting* for ever, even if it vested at once. Purpose trusts, it is said, must be so limited that they must end (it is not enough that they might end) within the perpetuity period, which usually meant twenty-one years, since there were no relevant lives, there being no individual beneficiaries. But charities are immune from this limit on duration. Charitable trusts can be perpetual.

MORTMAIN

But charities have not always had an unequivocal welcome from the state. Governments have long feared the accumulation of land in the hands of the church, and by the Mortmain statutes, which survived into this century, struck down many gifts of land to the church. 'Charitable and therefore void' is a well established judgment, even at the same time as the modern 'charitable and therefore valid' was being applied to other charities. The wide definition of religion in English courts probably reflects historically not so much a fundamental respect for human rights by the judges, as a desire to extend the mortmain net so that minor sects would come under the same forfeitures as the established church.

(b) Non-charitable purpose trusts for 'abstract' purposes

On the other hand, denying the charitable status of a purpose trust has in modern times been its death sentence. This judicial control is said to reflect another establishment fear, though this may be taken seriously for the first time only about the middle of this century. This is a fear of trusts set up for purposes which though not against public policy or in some way capricious, are nonetheless not sufficiently valuable to the community for it to be thought right for property to be tied up to support them. England might otherwise be like France, it was said, with a statue of a jumped-up politician in every town square. (Perhaps if French town squares had contained statues of jumped-up judges, if the fantasy be excused, things might have been different.) In an ingenious device to keep themselves out of having to evaluate such matters and to adjudicate upon good or bad, courts have taken to saying that a trust with no one to enforce it will fail. So unless a trust is charitable or is for individual beneficiaries, it cannot exist. This is the so-called 'beneficiary principle' which comes from a group of cases of which *Leahy v. Attorney-General for New South Wales* (1959) is the most important, and it virtually produced a rule of law that a purpose trust which was not charitable was of its very nature invalid. Examples would be trusts to promote world peace, or to promote particular non-'religious' philosophies, like anthroposophy. In keeping, however, with a judicial tenderness to that section of the table above the salt (reform of educational charity is another clear example), the courts did not erase a small group of abstract purpose trusts for a number of self-indulgent purposes, principally an obsession of the well-to-do, notably the maintenance of animals, graves and certain monuments. Before *Leahy* courts had been struggling with all sorts of objections; public policy, capriciousness, perpetuity, all of which would have been quite unnecessary if the fundamental truth of 'no trust without beneficiary' had been clearly seen. Nor is it so easy to see.

THE 'BENEFICIARY PRINCIPLE'

The Attorney-General is only in the oddest sense a beneficiary of a charitable trust, and only in the most artificial sense may we say that such a trust is enforced in his favour. But the maxim does emphasise one of the curiosities of the modern trust. Historically, trusts often originally arose in a context where testators wished to confer benefits on people other than their heirs. This could be done by the device of conditional conveyance at common law, but the problem is that the common law treated the condition as simple contract and would only let it be enforced by the parent's successor, the heir; the very person least likely to do so. The (contractual) right of enforcement could not be alienated to the person intended to be benefited. The Chancellor stepped in and gave enforcement rights to the third party beneficiary. But it became established (somewhat illogically?) as a consequence that the heir could not enforce, in Equity at any rate, even if he wanted to. This is odd since there appears to be no substantial mischief in having two groups of people able to enforce the trust, and it is easy to imagine situations where beneficiaries might be more concerned not to upset trustees than a settlor might be, and where alternative enforcement by an heir would thus prevent unconscionable conduct. Any administrative scruples one might have disappear in the case of purpose trusts which have no beneficiaries, and it is the settlor who enforces, or no one. Nor is it an objection that he might not bother: nor might beneficiaries in the standard institutional trust. But the courts appear to have set their faces against settlor-enforced trusts, at least if they arise so named. The courts will admit, first, trusts, where there must be beneficiaries or the

Attorney, and where control is vested in them alone; second, contracts for the benefit of third parties, where the control remains with the contracting parties, who retain the right of revocation, a useful alternative and an enrichment of the machinery of benefaction; and third, powers, where the objects can complain of misfeasance but cannot demand a transfer. The question which purpose trusts suggest is, 'Why not settlor-enforced trusts?' A disguised answer may be forthcoming. There have been two recent developments.

(c) Non-charitable purpose trusts which benefit individuals

The first has been to fine out a sub-set of non-charitable purpose trusts which do confer sufficient benefits on individuals to give them *locus standi* to enforce the trust. Such trusts are outside the mischief of the beneficiary principle and are thus valid. This appears to have been the contribution of *Re Denley* (1969), and it looked like a welcome addition to the range of options open to settlors. Provided the benefit was not too indirect or intangible and that the trust was not otherwise so framed as to exclude standing to sue, trusts for purposes which benefited individuals were to be permitted. Lord Simonds's remark in *Leahy* that a trust can be created for persons but not for purposes, seemed to have been sidestepped. Indeed, such trusts appear to have existed prior to this decision, but not to have been identified as such, the problem not having been spotted. So trusts to bury victims of disaster or to support named aged women or to pay creditors had all previously been held valid. We could now add a trust to provide a sports ground for employees of a company.

OPPOSITION
Recent judicial dicta have however cast some doubt on the *Denley* decision by asserting that it was simply a gift to individuals. It is not clear whether this assertion is merely a construction point – the judge did not read the document carefully enough and failed to spot that it was an ordinary discretionary trust; or a doctrine point – there is no separate category of purpose trusts which benefit individuals. No definition of terms has however been offered, and it is important to see what are the implications of asserting that such trusts do or do not exist.

The issue might arise in the following way, using as an example a familiar family problem and its solution. A trust to educate one's own children is not a charitable trust. Let us say that parents are contemplating what provision to make for their three children in the event of their death. Let us further imagine that one of the children is much older than the others, who are twins, and has been through a tertiary education at the expense of the parents. It is the parents' wish that each of their children should have the chance of this tertiary schooling and £25,000, and no more, as a testamentary gift. They make a will in which they provide for a sum of money, let us say £20,000, to be vested in trustees on trust to educate the twins to the end of tertiary education, if they shall not have reached this stage at the date of their deaths, and then make gifts of £25,000 each to the three children, with all residue going to their favourite charity. They both die while the twins, now eighteen years old, are still at school. The twins decide they would rather not go to college but would like to have the £10,000 each to buy a car, and they approach the trustees and demand their £10,000 in addition to the £25,000. The trustees know it was the parents' wish that this should not happen, but they are in a spot. If the gift is no more than a simple or discretionary gift to trustees on trust for the twins, in most common law jurisdictions the rule in *Saunders v. Vautier* (1841) gives persons absolutely entitled to a gift the right to demand payment of it either to themselves or at their direction. For instance, all the beneficiaries of a discretionary trust, if they can find each other (sometimes now impossible after *Re Baden*) and can all agree to direct the trustees what to do with the assets, may effectively destroy the discretion by directing the trustees what to do with the money. Likewise a so-called bare trust to a person payable at age thirty, where the trustees hold on trust for that person absolutely, may be terminated by that person demanding payment of the capital at any date after reaching adulthood. So if the trust to educate the twins can only be a gift of this sort, with simply an expressed preference that the money should be spent on education, the twins could demand the capital from the trustees and defeat the parents' wishes, and also the legitimate expectations of the charity. If, however, this is a non-charitable purpose trust for the benefit of an individual, where the education is part of the disposition, the trustees may be able, or indeed be obliged by the charity, to tell the twins that the gift is for education only and that if they wish to defeat that part of the gift by their own act, the £20,000 goes into residue. Whether the same result should follow if the frustrating event were not the result of a voluntary act of the beneficiary is not clear (see page 154 below). But what is clear is that the classification of such gifts is not a mere matter of labelling; it may affect beneficial entitlement, and writing mixed persons/purpose trusts out of the system may well impoverish it. The following account assumes that purpose trusts for non-charitable objects which benefit individuals are a separate category.

CERTAINTY IN 'MIXED' PERSONS/PURPOSES TRUSTS
There are two unanswered questions relating to these 'mixed' purpose trusts which arise in the light of recent developments in certainty law and in the law of perpetuities. First, how certain do the objects of such a mixed purpose trust have to be? As far as individuals are concerned, it would seem likely that the *Baden* test, whatever that now is, will be applied. Such trusts bear marked similarities to discretionary trusts since their execution will most often require the exercise of discretionary judgment by trustees. It is harder to fathom an answer to the question of how certain the purposes themselves will have to be. Here the threshold choice would seem to be whether to take the *Coxen* approach and weigh it all up in an impressionistic sort of way, or whether to adopt the *Broadway Cottages–Gulbenkian–Baden* approach and have a test – can you list all the possible purposes authorised by the document, or is it enough, for example, that you can say of any hypothetical purpose that it is or is not authorised? The courts have not left us with sufficient clues to solve this latter problem.

'MIXED' PURPOSE TRUSTS AND PERPETUITIES
The second question is what perpetuity regulation will be applied to this institution. There is, we guess, unlikely to be immunity from perpetuities. Purpose trusts will be subject to the vesting perpetuity rule, so they must begin in time, and to the rule against perpetual duration, which says they must so end. This is admittedly the law for the anomalous animals, graves and monuments group, which have been limited to an existence of twenty-one years. But the *Denley* type of trust may have found a loophole in the law. Since it was decided, most common law jurisdictions have reformed their perpetuity law by looking, as was mentioned above, not at possible, but at actual

events, and only if the interest has not in fact vested at the end of the perpetuity period will it fail. The rule against perpetual duration, which also looked at possible, not actual, events has not, however, been reformed in the UK, and so it remains the case of the anomalous group that if they are to be valid, it must be known from the beginning that they will terminate within the twenty-one-year period. But section 15(4) of the Perpetuities and Accumulations Act 1964 preserved the rule against perpetual duration in terms which suggest it is limited to the abstract, animal type trusts, but not for the new mixed type, which received articulated judicial recognition only after the statute was passed. Arguably, there is no perpetuity rule presently in existence for such trusts. There would seem to be two choices in keeping with the new mood. One would be to acknowledge the distinct similarity to discretionary trusts and to say that for the purpose of the perpetuity rule they would be so characterised. If the beneficiaries constitute a class, the new law is that if, under the terms of the gift, it is possible for new members to join the class after the end of the perpetuity period, then all parties identified as members of the class by that date take, and all future members are excluded. But this solution may make little sense in most cases of this sort. Take a trust to permit employees of a company to use land as a playing field. The purpose of having a perpetuity rule would be to limit the duration of the trust to the perpetuity period. The application of the class gift rule would be to vest the field in the employees absolutely at the end of the period, at the very moment when the law's policy should be to take it away from them. That is also likely to be the settlor's policy if he cannot have perpetuity. It might be possible, however, to achieve a sensible result by treating the gift as if it were a discretionary gift of income, valid from year to year for all objects identified up to the end of the perpetuity period.

An alternative solution is to turn to special powers of appointment, with which these mixed purpose trusts also have similarities. There is also an historical link. The old common law rule for these powers was that the power was void unless it was bound to be completely exercised within the perpetuity period. Since this rule was virtually identical in its formulation with the old rule against perpetual duration, it was at one time unsuccessfully argued that purpose trusts were really not trusts at all, but powers, and that the so-called rule against perpetual duration did not exist, being merely the ordinary application of the main rule against perpetuities to special powers. If treated as powers, these dispositions might have been valid, if limited to end within the perpetuity period, since powers are not vulnerable to the beneficiary principle, not being enforced in the same way. The rule for special powers has also been altered to a 'wait and see' philosophy by the statute, and it is now the law that special powers are valid insofar as they are in fact exercised within the period. So exercise is possible for the period only, at the end of which time the asset if still wholly or partly in existence, either goes on a gift over or falls back into residue. A judicial decision that special powers would be the model for perpetuity regulation of purpose trusts would not only maintain some historical continuity, but also produce a socially acceptable result.

'AN ABSTRACT PURPOSE TRUST BY ANY OTHER NAME'
A second development calls into question the whole theoretical foundation of this part of the law. It requires us to reconsider why the law has not permitted abstract purpose trusts and whether it should continue its hostility towards them. Plainly abstract purposes are being promoted in the community, with no harmful effect on our lives, and they are being permitted by legal devices of such dubious legitimacy that it might be asked why courts do not cast off the burden of precedent and address the fundamentals. The development has arisen in connection with an investigation into the nature of a gift to a particular political party, and it is in the context of gifts to organisations that the need for a new look has become most pressing. The enquiry is of analytical interest for it illustrates the ways in which contract can be used to mimic trust, and also raises the question of whether it is sensible of the law to prevent an aim being realised on policy grounds if it goes under one name, and then to allow it if it calls itself by another. It cannot be right that such a substantial part of the social life of the community should rest on such unsatisfactory foundations.

(d) Gifts to organisations

Organisations fall into three basic categories for the purpose of this discussion. They may be corporations; they may be unincorporated associations, which have no corporate existence and where the cement between the members is contractual, often called clubs; or they may be associations of a more loose structure where some of the members are joined by contract, but they are not all mutually bound by contract each to the other. A gift to a corporation causes no relevant problems. The corporation has personality and is itself an individual and the gift is generally like one to any individual. A gift to either of the other two, however, is much more complex. The only entity in these two cases is a social creature and though it may have a powerful social personality, there is no personality recognised by the law. 'It' cannot therefore be the transferee of a gift.

A GIFT TO A CLUB, OR ITS CHAIRMAN OR OTHER OFFICER

The beginning of all wisdom on this subject comes from *Leahy*: a gift to a club (or its chairman, or treasurer) creates a construction problem: the syntax of the gift creates a nonsense – there is no 'club' which the law can see, and the alternative, by identifying the donee by an office of this sort shows that the officer is not intended to take beneficially. The construction exercise is then to ask what, behind this 'strange' form of words, our donor intended. To discover this we have to look at the rest of the document and the other known facts about the donor and his relationship with the club. Once the gift has been construed, and the intention of the donor discovered, we move on to the second stage, which is to apply the appropriate rules of law. Starting with the matter of construction, the first question we would ask would be whether the gift was intended to be on trust for the purposes of the organisation. In this case the checklist is above: are the purposes charitable? If so, the gift is valid, subject to any perpetuity problem. If not, are the purposes abstract, or for the benefit of individuals? If the former, the gift will fail (unless within the excepted anomalous class, a difficult case to imagine); if the latter, it will have to obey the rules for the mixed trusts. If the gift is not for purposes, it must be to people only. On the present analysis, if the court finds that it was the intention of the donor that the members should be free to spend capital and income as they think fit, there cannot be a purpose trust. A range of possibilities now exists. In all of these possibilities there will almost inevitably be a bare trust. The legal estate or interest in the gift will vest in, say, a treasurer on bare trust for the members beneficially. It will be unusual in the extreme for a club to exist where the legal interest is vested in the whole membership, and in the case of gifts of land, legislation will usually now require a trust. But the trust will be a mere holding device: it will not itself determine how the asset is to be enjoyed. That will depend entirely on the wishes of those beneficially entitled, subject to the constraints we are about to reach. Although this discussion is in terms of gifts, which is the context in which the issue most often arises, similar considerations will apply to transfers made to the organisation for value.

(i) A gift to members beneficially

In the first place a gift 'to a club' might be construed as a gift to the individual members of the organisation beneficially. It would then become part of their individual assets and taken into account in any fiscal assessment of their worth. It would be theirs to spend as they individually wished. Such a construction of a gift would be extremely rare, and we might expect it to figure mainly in the case of small, very informal clubs which exist for the physical comfort of their members, like dining clubs. It can, and has been used also to by-pass one of the more unpleasant aspects of religious charity law, which excludes from charitable status contemplative orders like the Carmelites, by treating a gift to a house of such an order as a gift to its members beneficially, and relying on their consciences to ensure that it is not misspent. Such a gift might be intended in 'joint' form, in which case the interests of individual members will not be transmissible on death, but will pass to the remaining members of the group, the survivor taking what has not been spent; or it may be held 'in common', in which case the share of individual members will pass into their estates on death. In the case of joint interests, members can unilaterally transform their interests into interests in common, by performing so-called acts of severance. There is one variant of this construction which causes some difficulty because of recent observations made by judges, which can only be described as mistaken. The possibility is that the donor intended the gift to be to present and future members, and that our gift is so construed. Unless the donor limited the gift to members becoming ascertained within the perpetuity period, the old law, most clearly stated by Cross J in *Neville Estates v. Madden* (1962), said it was void for perpetuity. This rule has been repeated from the Bench recently, but it is hard to see how it can be other than a mechanical following of precedent without looking at its reasoning. A gift to present and future members is a gift to persons identified by a description, a class gift. The common law of perpetuity (with an exception that is not relevant in these situations) treated a class gift as a single gift for vesting purposes. It did not vest until all the members of the class qualified. So if it was possible that a single member would qualify outside the period, the whole gift failed and no one took anything. (Hard to defend.) What Cross J was saying was that a gift to present and future members of a club was a class gift; since (if?) it was possible that the club would still be in existence after the end of the perpetuity period, then the gift might vest outside the period and thus fail for everyone. But in that court, and many others, the law is now different. Class gifts do not now suffer from a unitary vesting concept. Since the 1964 Perpetuities and Accumulations Act we now wait until the end of the period. At that moment the class is closed and all those who are then members of it take their share, to the exclusion of all future members. The gift intended by the donor is in that sense partly good and partly bad. That is now the law for present and future members of a club. It will not fail from the beginning as it did before 1964. The problem is hardly likely to arise with any frequency: it is hard to imagine circumstances in which such a construction would recommend itself to a judge, though it could arise expressly.

(ii) 'Property subject to contract'

Secondly, the gift could be construed as a gift to the present members beneficially, but the donor could intend it to be held by them subject to the terms of a contract they had made with regard to its enjoyment, the constitution of the club, whatever those terms are. Again the members would have an absolute proprietary interest in their share, they would own their bit, but they would receive it only on terms that they subjected it to the contract which formed the constitution of the club, and which would therefore govern how it could be enjoyed. This notion of something I own, but which I ought to use only according to a contract I have made with you, is a familiar one outside clubland. Its application inside clubs is, however, rather special. If the parties have actually made a contract, its express terms will govern, but the courts will also supply terms which the parties have not made explicit, a common and valuable feature of judicial technique. But the implied terms which the courts have used in these cases are so extraordinary that one might hail the birth of the 'constructive contract'. The contract seems to operate, in the absence of any express provision to the contrary, in the following way. Each member takes initially a proportionate share of any gift made by the donor, and will have an equitable proprietary interest in it. The contract determines this proportionate share not by taking a simple head count, but by looking first at the amount of subscription paid by the member and then dividing up the assets on a head count equally amongst members paying the same subscription. So a member paying £10 a year will take twice as much as a member paying £5 a year. Each member is also deemed to have contracted with fellow members that any other assets, such as existing capital assets or subscriptions, are held on the same terms, and the contract will perform an instant levelling operation on each new asset as it comes in, distributing it evenly amongst the members in the same shares. When a member dies or leaves the club, he contracts to leave all his share to the surviving members at the date of resignation or death. Any new member of the organisation will, on joining, acquire a share in the club's assets proportionate only to the amount of his subscription rate, not according to how long he has been a member. So all members paying the same subscription have the same beneficial interest in the 'club's property'. No member can withdraw any of this property, however, except in accordance with the terms of the contract, which will normally require the consent of other members. The officers will be permitted to apply the property to the purposes of the club as authorised by the contract and each such act of expenditure will proportionately deplete the share of each member. There is a special term in this contract that the contract can be varied by a majority of its members. It is not yet clear whether this remarkable construct also contains 'minority shareholder protection' clauses, so that a sectional majority cannot appropriate part or all of the assets for their own selfish purposes. The contract thus sits, computer-like, at the centre of the club's world, making instant calculations and dispositions of the club's property.

This 'property subject to contract' regime should perhaps be established by statute. It is hard, however, to fit it into existing rules of law. A number of elementary difficulties arise, quite apart from the rather obvious over-exercise of judicial imagination, in creating the scheme. If members of the club are not adult, they can hardly be prevented from walking out with their shares, since minors cannot be bound by such contracts; yet clubs containing minors appear to be deemed to be run in the same way. And since all the movements of beneficial interests amount to 'dispositions', statute, as we shall see, renders them void unless made in writing (Law of Property Act 1925, section 53(i)(c)), which of course they almost never are. Nor is it clear how the contracts are thought to be enforced. Since what the contract agrees shall be done is assumed by this device actually to have happened, it seems that at least the contracts are thought to be specifically enforceable (and then applying the 'Equity treats as done' rule to them). How such simple commercial contracts attract such a remedy remains unexplained. Finally, the way in which this contract is formed, between parties who never meet and may even be unaware of each other's existence, is obscure, though some application of the disingenuous common law rule that allows members of, say, a regatta, who may also never have met, to sue each other in contract, might come to the rescue (*Clarke v. Dunraven*, 1897).

(iii) 'Clubs' with no unifying contract: mandate theory

But what if we cannot construe it as a gift to members beneficially and we are faced with an organisation whose social cohesion is achieved by some contractual linking, but whose structure is so complex that all its members are not bound to each other by a shared single contract? Perhaps clubs with some infant members should also be transferred to this category. Plainly the previous constructions are not now open to the courts. In a recent case of a large political party, which did indeed have a series of contractual arrangements, but whose final cohesion was purely social, all the constructions mentioned so far were impossible, and the court was faced with the awesome possibility that gifts to it could not be made because the machinery for describing or administering them did not exist. It has risen to the occasion by introducing the concept of mandate into this debate. This case might be thought to have raised in an acute form how far the courts should go in exercising their imaginations and inventing constructs which are neither legally convincing nor even bona fide attempts to construe the gift. The case was *Conservative and Unionist Central Office v. Burrell* (1982). A gift to a large political party is most naturally seen as a gift on trust to promote its purposes. It is not a gift to its members beneficially in any shape or form. Trusts for political purposes are not charitable, nor do they benefit their members within the meaning of the rules discussed above. The trust would thus be an abstract purpose trust and void under the beneficiary principle. In the *Burrell* case Brightman LJ came to the rescue with the opinion that when I give money to the Conservative Party, I am simply giving the Treasurer of the party a mandate, a contractual arrangement, which *permits* him to spend the money on the purposes of the party. At this point we have what might also be described as a purpose power, if such exists, operating perhaps entirely at common law. If the Treasurer now mixes my money with the other funds of the party, my mandate becomes irrevocable. I can never get my money back. I can stop him from applying my money for other non-party purposes (though since this is contract, I cannot sue his successors). More importantly, since this is contract, it is not easy to see how such an arrangement can be made by will, since a contract of agency cannot be set up at the moment of death. Rather oddly, at the end of a judgment that is almost entirely *obiter*, Brightman LJ refers to this problem, opining that its solution is not difficult, but declines to prejudge its resolution by letting us into the secret. So gifts by will to the Conservative Party await their legal justification.

THE WAY FORWARD?

Burrell is the case that most gives this game away. Towards the end of the judgment comes the sentence, 'No contributor to Central Office funds will view his contribution in this way . . . he believes he is making an out and out contribution or gift to a political party.' The exercise has thus changed its juridical nature since *Leahy*; it is no longer a construction, in the sense of construing; it has become a construction in the sense of constructing. We are not looking at what the donor intends, but trying to fit his intentions into a legal framework that works, whether or not it approximates to the category he has in mind. It is in this sense like the worst kind of affiliation proceedings, trying to father off the gift on the nearest doctrine that will support it. And of course it does not work. The 'property subject to contract' device for clubs is riddled with difficulties (see page 155), and the mandate theory not only seems to fail in terms of which Treasurer I can sue and whether I can make such a deal in my will, but also fails lamentably in giving effect to my intention, if its operation will not afford me an action to force the Treasurer to spend my money on the purposes of the party. As it stands at present it resembles a constructed purpose power. In the period when the beneficiary principle was being formulated, counsel pleaded with courts to give effect to purpose trusts as purpose powers, which did not attract the defeating operation of the principle. The courts then refused, and this case in effect, though not in form, marks a reversal of that policy. It is also quite clear that in the club cases, the courts are allowing purposes to be effectuated under the cloak of a contractual apparatus, which they would strike down if they came honestly out into the open as purpose trusts. For it is certainly the case that a gift to such a club whose purposes are, say, antivivisection, will be applied for those purposes for so long as there are people who care about live experiments: a living purpose trust, so to speak. A purpose trust for antivivisection purposes would be void under the beneficiary principle. One answer would simply be to borrow from contractual thinking and permit settlor-enforced trusts in the case of abstract purposes. Like club members holding under the property-subject-to-contract theory, the settlor might not maintain the purpose, in which case the capital would accumulate for the twenty-one-year perpetuity period which seems to have been agreed for abstract purpose trusts, when it would pass on to those entitled to the gift over. And since we do not exercise much control over the contractual purposes of clubs, we could afford to be a little more relaxed about the control of purposes in purpose trusts. And who can doubt but that in the cases of gifts to unincorporated associations, or to organisations like the Conservative Party, enforcement for a purpose is what the donor wants, and if the law will give it to him under one name, on ramshackle contractual theory, why not take the bull by the horns and re-examine the bases of the objections to non-charitable abstract purpose trusts?

7

Settling the Subject Matter

1. INTRODUCTORY

POLICY

This is one of the areas where Equity is most clearly seen to be working out the detailed implications of the property law it invented to order the moral obligations of the trustee. It is very much practitioners' law in the sense that much of the material comes from operations in which lawyers have had a formative hand and which have not been produced on kitchen tables. It is redolent with the values of administrative effectiveness and consistency. Lawyers need to be able to plan and advise before these transactions are undertaken, and certainty keeps costs of all sorts to a minimum. Changing the law to make provision for individual hardship in this area is therefore particularly difficult. The judge may do 'justice' to the individual before him, and injustice to large numbers outside the court whose settled planning and legitimate expectations are thrown into question by the introduction of discretionary justice, or even simple change. Most judges, most of the time, recognise this awesome responsibility to the parties who are not before them.

INCENTIVES TO ANALYSIS

Tax and formalities have played a major part in developing this part of the law. A formality, or formal requirement, is some legal prerequisite of validity, not forming part of the substantive definition of the transaction to which it is attached. Identical formalities may thus be attached to a wide range of legal transactions without affecting their substantive nature. Writing, or the requirement of a sealed writing, or deed, are good examples of legal formalities. (A deed might in fact be said to be the most perfect formality; easy to make intentionally, and virtually impossible to make by accident.) The need for property, certain objects and intention to create a trust, for example, are not formalities but are part of the concept of the trust. It is not always easy to say when deeds are used as formalities and when as substance. To take a common law example: land and chattels were originally only to be transferred by delivery; the rule has a basic appeal to the very notion of what a delivery is. If we say you need a deed as well, deeds are formalities. But what if we say you can use a deed instead? Since nothing turns on that in this part of Equity, we can leave it here as a puzzle, and will treat deeds, as do the books, as a formality. The formalities we are concerned with have their modern origin in statute, but this is simply coincidence. Handshakes might be regarded as formalities in the world of business morality. Where there are no formalities the need for legal analysis is much reduced. If a transaction is valid as one of a number of possibilities, it will not much matter which one it is. But if one of the possibilities has a formal requirement for validity, and another not, it may suddenly become crucial to know which one it is. Since most major transactions are in any event now done in writing – a common formal requirement – the analytical effect of formalities is to a degree reduced. But put a tax on a written document if it is one kind of transaction, and not if it is another, and all of a sudden we are back in the textbooks. Real people's money in a real world will depend on who best has understood the analytical effect of what has been done. It is in this way that the Inheritance Tax in the UK is likely to give a stimulus to 'old-fashioned' black letter analysis of this kind, depending as it does on the traditional learning of the Chancery.

TRANSFERS OR GRANTS, AND CONTRACTS

According to a long tradition in Western Europe, based on common sense if nothing more, if you want to alter proprietary relations, you have to perform an act in the law of property. It is not enough to intend to do so, to agree to do so, or unilaterally to promise to do so, and especially not to have wished that you had done so. Common law and Equity both start from this standpoint, though Equity has a small number of exceptions, and in particular is willing to reward those who score ten out of ten for effort. The three basic acts available to us in this property world are *transfer*; *transfer to trustees on trust*; and *declaration of trust*, where the declaror constitutes or makes himself a trustee of property in which he previously had a beneficial title. We may *promise or agree* to do any of these acts, and we may do so *for value* or *gratuitously*. This at once trebles the three cases with which we began, but this is only the simple beginning, and the first task facing any lawyer dealing with this topic, known as constitution of trusts, is to identify which of the situations is under consideration. In particular it is crucial to distinguish between performing the proprietary act and agreeing or promising to do so, though here, as we shall again see, 'Equity treating as done etc.' has blurred the simple distinction, causing agreement to behave like grant. This is also the one subject where the penalties of trying to run before you can walk are most savage. Built up in easy stages, this is a fascinating puzzle; rushed at, it has all the analytical attractiveness of a bowl of spaghetti. Although the law is not, in a most fundamental sense, a game, in areas like this it bears its most striking similarity to one.

2. TRANSFER

This notion is one shared by both law and Equity. It goes under many other generic names, including 'grant' or 'disposition'. Its central effect is that the proprietary interest vested in the transferor becomes vested in the transferee, the transferor retaining nothing of what has been transferred. The language has become a little specialised. Transfer of land has come to be called conveyance; choses in action are 'assigned' using either equitable rules or those of statute, and we talk about the assignment or disposition of equitable interests; shares in a company are 'transferred' using the machinery of the companies legislation. Although there is some dispute on the matter concerning the assignment of choses in action, contractual debts for example, in principle, if the transferor has the intention of transferring the proprietary interest to the transferee, it does not matter whether the transfer is made for value or not. This is certainly the modern position for the (sometimes) so-called 'choses in Equity', rights which never had an existence at common law, like beneficiaries' interests under a trust. We will first look at formalities on transfers by the living, leaving formalities in wills to the next section.

Formalities

(a) TRANSFERRING A LEGAL INTEREST AMONGST THE LIVING

Transfers of shares and statutory assignments of choses in action are subject to the formality of writing. Transfers of interests in land will often be governed by the formal requirements of registration systems: where not, legal estates in land must by statute (with a limited exception for certain short leases) be transferred by deed (Law of Property Act 1925, sections 52, 54(2)). Chattels may be transferred by simple delivery (i.e. no formal requirement) or by deed. Dispositions of equitable interests must be in writing (Law of Property Act 1925, section 53(i)(c)).

The transfer may be of a legal proprietary interest transferred in a way which is effective at law, in which case the transferor ceases to have any interest and the transferee takes what the transferor had. If the legal estate was not encumbered with a trust, and if no new ground of intervention is raised on the circumstances of the transfer, this is absolutely nothing to do with Equity, and no equitable interest is transferred or involved. Beneficial title is perfectly well secured by the common law rules. Similarly, a transfer of a bare legal estate from one trustee to another will be a common law matter, though the transfer only affects who is trustee and not who can enjoy, and Equity will take an interest to see that the retiring trustee has safeguarded the position of the beneficiaries and to transfer his duties to the new trustee. A transfer of the legal estate by a trustee under the *Pilcher v. Rawlins* doctrine is a variant of this, but wiping out the equitable interest of the beneficiary under the trust as it goes; the bona fide purchaser takes only a legal estate, but it is now a beneficial legal estate, whereas his transferor had only a trustee's non-beneficial estate. This, as we discovered earlier, is a consequence of constitutional law doctrine and does not owe its theory to private law thinking – the jurisdictional split modifying the system. But in some cases where the act by a common law owner is not sufficient under common law statutory rules to pass the legal title, the transfer may yet be recognised in Equity, if it is for value. In this case the legal title will stay where it was, with the would-be transferor becoming a trustee, and a new equitable title will be created in the person to whom the transfer purported to be made. This is often called an equitable transfer; in fact since the transferor did not have an equitable title, it is an act of creation, Equity treating it as unconscionable for the transferor to retain the benefit of the legal title which he has retained, and it begins to resemble our third case, that of declaration of trust. We shall reach this in the section on agreements, which is the mechanism through which Equity achieves this result.

(b) TRANSFERRING AN EQUITABLE INTEREST AMONGST THE LIVING

Or the transfer may be of an equitable interest alone. Here the rules of common law have no sway since, by definition, if they recognised the interest, there would have been no need for Equity to have created it in the first place. Examples of this kind of transfer are where a beneficiary under a trust transfers his equitable interest – either a proprietary interest in the assets, or his rights to due administration of the trust against the trustees – directly to a third party, giving that party the same rights as the beneficiary previously had. This is an outstanding example of where a combination of tax law and formalities law has caused us to refine our understanding of the machinery. Consider the simple situation of a trustee, Y, holding on a bare trust for a single adult beneficiary, X. The trustee in such a case (or nominee, as he is sometimes called) has no duties to perform other than to hold the property and its yield on trust for X, and must obey any lawful instruction which X gives to him in respect of that property.

If X wishes to transfer the economic benefit in the property to Z, she has, if she does not wish to involve any new party, two choices. She could either

(i) assign her equitable interest to Z; or

(ii) she could declare herself trustee of the equitable interest for Z, creating a sub-trust, as it is called.

She could also agree or promise to do either of these two, for value or not. But if we remain with the proprietary choices, if she declares herself trustee she will have asset-stripped the equitable interest which she had at the beginning of the story, turning it into a bare equitable interest and conferring on Z the benefits from the interest, vested in herself. It is thus clear that not only are all beneficial interests not equitable interests (many legal interests are beneficial), but that not all equitable interests are beneficial (they may be held on trust for another). The first choice constitutes an assignment of an equitable interest and must be in writing if the title is to reach Z since it is a 'disposition of an equitable interest' within the meaning of the Law of Property Act 1925, section 53(i)(c). The second is a declaration of trust and needs no writing unless the subject matter is land, in which case section 53(i)(b) of the same Act requires writing. So far, what X knows is that if she does the first, and if there is a law which levies a tax on instruments which dispose of equitable interests, she will have to pay the tax. She rejects the second option because she does not wish to have any further involvement with these assets, which that device might involve. We will return to it.

X therefore decides that what she will do is neither of these, but a third which, like the first, will keep her from the possibility of personal trusteeship, and which she also hopes will operate directly in a property world (and save her the tax). She

(iii) directs the trustee, Y, to hold on new trusts for Z absolutely. This is neither a simple transfer nor a declaration of trust, and the question is whether it is outside the formalities rules about 'dispositions' and can therefore effectively be done orally. Can X simply orally tell Y what to do?

FUNCTIONS OF THE FORMALITIES RULES: DISPOSITIONS

A court would have a choice of taking a strict formal view ('not a simple transfer'), in which case oral validity would be the result, or a broader and functional approach to the formalities rules, in which case it might not. The first issue, then, is why, in this corner of the law, do we have formalities rules? The answer seems to be as it should be in trust law, to protect the trustee by leaving him a paper trail which he can follow, to allow him best to determine for whose benefit he should hold and administer the trust property. If a stranger approaches him and claims to be a replacement beneficiary, he should not have to rely only on the stranger's report of an oral dealing. In an ideal world, the former beneficiary who made the disposition ought also to be made to inform the trustee (a model used in the assignment of choses in action, and toyed with for equitable interests under trusts at the beginning of the nineteenth century), so that the trustee does not make payments to the former beneficiary and so lay himself open to an action for a second payment by the new beneficiary; but this is not required for simple interests under trusts (though only a small development in negligence-type thinking could in some circumstances impose a liability on the assigning beneficiary – a beneficiary's duty to a trustee which would not be hard to defend on policy grounds). At least there will be a piece of paper. A further function of writing will be for trustees also to leave paper trails for their successors. It is undesirable that new trustees should rely on reports of oral conversations at one or more removes and not to have writings made by assignors.

The issue in our third case faced the court in *Grey v. IRC* (1958–60). The facts were in all relevant respects similar to those we are now considering: X directs her nominee Y to hold on new trusts for Z. The decision was that such a direction was sufficiently similar to a simple disposition to be caught by the writing requirement. How would we defend or attack such a decision? X no longer has her equitable interest; Z, although he does not technically have what X had, since X has destroyed her interest (thereby, as some might think, in that split second depriving herself of the right to give instructions to Y), does have an interest sufficiently similar to X's former interest for us to regard Z as having what X once had. We may not need to protect Y by insisting on writing, since to effect this device, X must actually talk to Y, so Z cannot be the stranger to Y we hypothesised earlier. But it might be thought to be good policy to insist that X should initially produce her own paper setting out the trusts for the benefit of Y's successors, so that they do not have to rely either on oral conversations, or on writings made only by Y. So the decision is a half measure, both in analytical and functional terms.

But there are many more strings to X's bow, if she does not like the result in method three. She could simply

(iv) direct her trustee, Y, to transfer the legal estate to Z in such a way as to make him full beneficial owner. Once X has made the transfer, there is no longer a trust. Z is beneficial owner at law, and has no equitable interest. There has not therefore been a disposition of an equitable interest; it has been destroyed. Functionally, writing is unnecessary because there is no longer a trustee, Y having no assets and being discharged, and there being no possibilities of successor trustees. The House of Lords got this right (they will be pleased to hear) on both counts in *Vandervell v. IRC* in 1967, holding that such a direction could be made orally. Which is perhaps as well, because it has implications for the ubiquitous *Pilcher v. Rawlins*. The version just recited is in proprietary terms identical to a *Pilcher v. Rawlins* operation. The only difference is that in that case the trustee, by conveying the legal estate to a bona fide purchaser for value without notice, commits a wrong against his beneficiaries, for which, if he can be found, he must pay; in the *Vandervell* case, the trustee who is conveying the legal estate to one he knows will not take it as trustee, is behaving lawfully. No one has ever suggested that a bona fide purchaser of a legal estate for value without notice takes free of the interest of the beneficiaries only if the transfer to him was in writing. The equitable interest of X has been 'disposed of' in the sense of being destroyed, but it has not been the subject matter of a disposition. Murderers may dispose of their victims, but they do not make dispositions of them. At this point we should remind ourselves why the beneficial legal owner of a chattel can transfer beneficial title of it to another common law owner without writing – he has no equitable interest to start with, and the transferee does not end up with one either.

We now have three characteristics of the 'disposition' of an equitable interest. There must be a trust in existence at the beginning of the transaction; there must be a trust in existence at the end of it; and the new beneficiary must have what the former beneficiary in substance had. The ink had not dried, however, on the judgment/speeches in the House of Lords in *Grey* (indeed it is said not even to have been written) before the profession thought it had found the answer, number five.

(v) X, having a beneficial legal title, conveys shares to Y as nominee for herself, and at the same time gives Y the power to declare new beneficial interests. Y, subsequently having had a friendly nudge from his old friend and client X, thinks it right in the exercise of his own unfettered discretion to declare new trusts, making Z sole beneficiary. (Such coincidences – Z is just the person X would have chosen – are commonplace in the administration of discretionary trusts where the puppet master is often the settlor, who has in theory dropped out. A good example of Equity not practising what it preaches, and looking at the form, not the substance.) Does Y have to declare new trusts in writing? It seems to be believed that he does not, perhaps on the basis that this is, or is sufficiently like, a declaration of trust, though a declaration by a trustee is hardly a paradigm declaration of trust. The result might then be different if the subject matter were land, as we shall see. If so, we have to add a further limb to our definition of a disposition: it must be made by one beneficiary in favour of another, and since Y is not beneficially entitled, merely having the power to affect the beneficial entitlement of others, this operation is exempt. As in *Grey*, too, the trustee knows who the new beneficiary is, so there is no functional difficulty at that point; but there will be no document for Y's successors, of which, this time, Y is the appropriate draftsman. A development of negligence-type liability might also be the answer here, but at the moment successors do not look well protected by the theory. In practice, no problems, no doubt, till someone forgets to tell a successor. . . . It should be noted that, as we shall see later, the *Grey* reasoning will need modification if the dealings are for value.

Formalities for transfer on death are best dealt with among transfers to trustees on trust, where they raise the most interesting problems.

THE TRANSFER-PROPERTY DEPENDENCY
Transfers can only operate over property. This is the link-up with the section on subject matter, mentioned earlier. In particular the problem which has caused most difficulty in this respect has been that of future property. We are indebted to two cases from Australia and New Zealand, decided virtually simultaneously in 1965, *Williams v. CIR* and *Shephard v. CIT*, for a clear statement of the simple truth that that which does not presently exist cannot presently be the subject matter of a property dealing of any of the three main kinds we are here considering. So income from a fund cannot be transferred, as it is not yet in existence. Past income, already in the bank, may be, as may the right to receive income, which is itself an existing right. We may settle the tree but not the fruit it has yet to bear. We may even settle branches on the tree, by assigning the right to people in shares (via trustees only in this case). We may also assign something as uncertain-looking as a life interest in the same way, provided it is the right we assign and not the contemplated yield. Even a joint share in a bank account may be assigned, provided that

it is the rights against the bank that are transferred and not what is left in the account at a future date, even though the effect is identical. The settlement must be of the fluctuating and defeasible asset, the rights against the bank, and not of the proceeds of that right. The crucial point is that if the right is assigned, the beneficiary may get nothing under the assignments if the right does not yield anything, and it is a major drawback of this rule that one cannot predict in known cash value terms what the beneficiaries will receive. In cases like this the 'game' element is most prominent – the law is happy for the act to be done, but doctrine says it must be done in a particular fashion, and it imposes some penalties along the way for the overambitious.

NO RECHARACTERISATION

The game element does, of course, appear less tolerable when the 'wrong' result is reached in an individual case, especially when the parties are not legally advised, and even more especially where such cases may represent a continuing category. Law of longstanding authority from the nineteenth century says that construction of what was intended is what matters, and that the court will not recharacterise the way in which a gift is made if it could have been done in one of several ways and the settlor chose one, which he then failed correctly to execute. So if one purports to make a gift by transfer of a legal estate in land, such as a lease, and omits to execute a deed; or fails to deliver chattels (not a formal defect) or make a deed of gift of them; or fails to endorse a cheque made payable to oneself, the would-be beneficiary takes nothing. In particular, the court will not recharacterise so that the transaction becomes a declaration of trust, even if by so doing it could save the gift. What courts ought to be doing in such circumstances is not obvious: one's sympathy for lay benefactors is in direct conflict with the efficiency needs of the professionals. Distinctions between the concepts are important, and running them together impoverishes the system. It also makes them less reliable where for tax reasons, say, one needs to use one of them, and the courts have made two of them indistinguishable in their formation characteristics. Perhaps the occasional litigant-sacrifice needs to be made to encourage people to take legal advice when undertaking transactions of this sort (though if the sacrifice cannot be publicized, it loses much of its value); and there is a value in discouraging incompetence. On the other hand, some of the talk in these cases is rather reminiscent of talk about 'maintaining the boundaries of actions at common law' – a value the abolition of which we have survived without obvious ill effect. And an alternative ground of validity – treating the would-be benefactor as himself trustee – was objected to in a different social world. Imposing the duties of a trustee on the benefactor, when he wanted to be rid of the property altogether, might have been thought to be burdensome on him. This rather 'gentlemanly' fear (trustees as 'players') looks a little exaggerated today, and in any event one should ask whether, if we did find a declaration of trust, we could not find that its only terms made it a special kind of bare trust which the trustee could, if he wished, insist on terminating by making a conveyance to the beneficiary. We should beware of thinking that all declarations of trust, especially constructive ones as these would be, have to be of the institutional model. If we are seeking intention, the obvious economic intention here is to be rid of the property, and one might ask how conscionable it truly is for the would-be transferor to retain the benefit, and if not, why his successors (who are the normal parties to the cases) should be in a better position. One might also ask what this kind of incompetent settlor would prefer: to see the gift fail as attempted, or to have it rescued as something else. It may be that in this highly practitioner-based area, we are expecting intentions of benefactors to be far too refined, and we may be expecting them to make distinctions they not only had never dreamt of, but might not even understand if they were explained. Their paramount intention might simply be to benefit. Finally, the attitude of strict adherence to principles of construction in this case should be contrasted with the creative recharacterisation approach in the club cases, of which *Conservative CO v. Burrell* (1982) is perhaps the best example.

EFFORT REWARDED

The nearest this subject comes to the *Burrell* approach is in the 'every best effort' doctrine. This doctrine is derived from an observation of Turner LJ in *Milroy v. Lord* (1862). It states that if the settlor has done everything in his power to transfer a title, it will not be foiled because a third party has not, or has not yet, done some act which is needed in order to make the transfer legally binding. The doctrine is expressed to be applicable to all three of our principal modes of settlement, but in practice can only be applied to two: this class and that of transfer to trustees on trust, where it operates identically. So, for example, a registered proprietor of land who has submitted the appropriate documents to the land registry will have done all that he could. Until the Registrar registers the intended donee as registered proprietor, the transferor will under this doctrine hold the legal estate on trust for the transferee. In other words, the transaction will be recharacterised as a declaration of trust. This doctrine is perhaps unobjectionable as a device where the third party, as is the case with the land registry, is obliged to register the transaction; but it is less clearly well founded where the third party is under no such obligation, as would be the case if the subject matter of the transfer were shares in a private company, where the directors are under no obligation to register the transfer of the shares into the name of the new proposed transferee. In that case the transferor may be forever left as trustee, when he had no such intention, in clear contravention of the rules stated above. It is perhaps significant that the case *Re Rose* (1952) (a case of transfer to trustees on trust, but that seems to make no difference), which decided that these old 'no recharacterisation' objections were not valid, even in the case of the private company, was a tax case, where if the transfer took effect only when the company registered the transfer, as it in fact did, tax was payable, but if the transferor had divested himself of the beneficial interest at the earlier date when he sent off the papers, tax would not be due. So the arbitrary deviation from principle results in non-payment of tax in a situation where applying the law would have resulted in such a payment. It has even, somewhat amazingly, been defended on just these grounds. This is not a unique example of the tax game, where the court moves the goalposts in favour of the taxpayer after the ball has been kicked.

OTHER CONCESSIONS

There are two other exceptions to the principle that the donor must execute a completed act if the gift is to take effect, both connected with the death of the donor, where an imperfect conveyance or even an intended conveyance will be completed in the donee's favour. These are where an intended donee is made the would-be donor's executor (possibly also where he is administrator), based perhaps on an old common law idea that executors were beneficially entitled to residue (the rule in *Strong v. Bird*, 1874); or else the gift is made conditionally in contemplation of death, the so-called *donatio mortis causa* (gift by reason of death) where, for sensible policy reasons connected with the circumstances in which these gifts are often made, the law has adopted relaxed delivery rules. A third possible exception is the law relating to estoppel, where would-be transferors may be prevented from denying the effect of incompleted gifts or even, rarely, forced to complete them. The basis of this part of the law has shifted rapidly in the last generation. It is dealt with in land law books since it appears to be confined in its operation to interests in land (famous last words department).

3. TRANSFER TO TRUSTEES ON TRUST

IRREVOCABILITY ON TRANSFER

Transfers to trustees on trust share some of the characteristics of the simple (!) transfers discussed above. A most striking example of similarity is in the rules governing revocability. At common law a gift, once delivered, is irrevocable, even though there was no obligation to make it in the first place. This was true even though the transferor had relied on protestations of friendship by the transferee which turned out to be misplaced, or even if the transferor had a run of financial disasters immediately after delivery and it was obvious to everyone that he would not have made the gift had he foreseen the future. So at common law, the rule seems to be: if in doubt, don't give. Equity appears to have followed the law in this entirely. Transfers of equitable interests by way of gift are likewise irrevocable. And treating the trustee as a mere manager, it has treated delivery to a trustee as completion, just as, at common law, delivery to the donee completed the gift. The trust is said to be constituted when the trustee gets the property, and not before. If there have been no promises (which we shall come to later), until that moment the would-be beneficiaries have nothing; once that moment is passed, the settlor has nothing. Indeed, if one takes the judges at their word, delivery to the trustee is both a necessary and a sufficient condition of constituting a trust in this fashion. That is, if transfer to Y on trust for X is what I intend, accidental delivery to X will not do. All sorts of lovely complications seem possible if, for instance, the settlor mistook X for Y and then died, and his estate sued X for return; or where X in these circumstances hands the asset to Y before he can be stopped, and where tax is deductible if the trust is constituted on the date when Y received it, but not if it is constituted when the asset is delivered to X. The position gets even more fascinating if the (intended) trust for X is a bare trust of the kind we have just been discussing, so that he can instantly demand the asset back from Y. The issue will then clearly raise a form/substance debate at a high level.

THE TRANSFER-PROPERTY DEPENDENCY AGAIN

It follows from what was said above about the invalidity of present transfers of future property, that if X purports to transfer, by way of gift to Y on trust, property to which he is not entitled at the moment of the purported transfer, the act is a nullity. The settlor is not making a promise, which might have some future reference, but is performing an act which simply fails. If the property then at some future date falls into the hands of X by virtue of his being chosen as trustee of another settlement under which the future property falls into X's hands (as can happen when families regularly choose the same people to be trustees of all their settlements), the earlier assignment, being simply a nullity, will not catch it. The settlor keeps it, as in *Re Brooks* (1939). Nothing has happened. On first principles the decision in this case seems absolutely right. The position would be different if he had *promised* to settle future property, and especially if he had so promised for value. A doctrine which is in some state of confusion at present also says that in some circumstances, not present in *Brooks*, failed transfers will take effect as contracts to transfer. We shall reach it shortly.

Formalities

(a) TRANSFER TO TRUSTEES OF LEGAL INTERESTS AMONGST THE LIVING

Take first the position of a beneficial legal owner making such a transfer. The rules for the transfer of the legal estate are as above. The equitable interest which is being created must be so created in writing if the subject matter is land (Law of Property Act 1925, section 53(i)(a)) but writing is not needed if it is personalty or chattels, since there is no disposition of an equitable interest (no trust to begin with), and no other provision imposes formal requirements. So a trust of chattels may be constituted by a beneficial legal owner entirely without formalities: the settlor can deliver them to the trustees and orally communicate the trusts. Successors of the trustees are again not protected, but this time by the clearest provisions (or absence of them) in the statutes. There is also one bizarre possibility. If it is a correct reading of the run of recent cases, of which *Gartside v. IRC* (1968) is an exemplar, that beneficiaries under a discretionary trust, for example, do not have an interest *in* the trust property (under section 53(i)(a)) but only rights *against* the trustees for due administration, the possibility arises of a discretionary trust of land, say a block of flats with separate titles or a scattered collection of houses, which escapes the formalities section mentioned because that section talks of interests *in* land, and the wider language of 'trusts respecting any land' is only in section 53(i)(b), which deals with declarations of trust, which we shall deal with next. (There is no point having a separate subsection on 'declarations', if they are covered by the 'created or disposed of' provisions of section 53(i)(a).)

(b) TRANSFER TO TRUSTEES OF EQUITABLE INTERESTS AMONGST THE LIVING

The transferor may not, however, have a legal interest. If she has an equitable interest, it seems she can now do two things with it and still remain within this section. She can:

(i) transfer it to a third party on trust for a fourth; X, who is a beneficiary of a trust of which Y is trustee, transfers her equitable interest to Y2 on trust for Z. Is this a disposition of an equitable interest and so needing writing? The income arising in Y's hands must now be paid to a new recipient, Y2, who holds it on trust for Z. Y2 now holds what X had, though it is now a non-beneficial equitable trust interest, and Y needs telling in writing so that he can check when Y2 makes his demands. It should be a disposition on grounds of substantial similarity, and on functional grounds it should need writing. But

(ii) X can also make her transfer back, as it were, to Y, her own trustee, on trust for Z beneficially. Y would now seem to have in sequence acquired a legal estate on trust for X, followed by X's beneficial interest on trust for Z. What must happen is that X's beneficial interest is destroyed, and Y now holds directly on trust for Z. Destruction of X's interest is not a disposition of it; Y knows what he is to do (though his successors need writing signed by someone). But there is a trust at the beginning and end, and Z gets substantially what X once had. Authority, in the shape of *Re Tyler's Fund Trusts* (1967), says it does need writing, but, entering into the spirit, says the writing need not mention Z.

(c) TRANSFERS TO TRUSTEES BY THE DEAD

It is rumoured that a great European (in the insular sense) civilian lawyer of the last century once remarked that a will was a disposition of property by a person who could not make a disposition, over property he did not own. Be that as it may, the two pressures of a need to defeat the stranglehold of male primogeniture over land, and the mortal desire to provide what was satirically described as 'fire insurance', by making pious gifts, produced an irresistible coalition for the recognition of a power to control the future disposition of property at the moment of death. If ever there was an area needing regulation by formalities, however, that area was this area. When a will came up for consideration, the principal actor would be missing, and the sort of questions of intent and coercion which instantly come to mind seem almost insoluble if we allow oral wills in any but the most intimate societies. Some device was also needed to prevent drafts of wills being mistaken for final testaments. Statutes, therefore, beginning with the great Statute of Frauds of 1677, have provided that no will shall be valid unless it is in writing, signed by the testator and witnessed. This is the case whatever the subject matter – there are no special rules for land or personalty, choses in possession or choses in action. There are therefore no exceptions in the statute for constructive trusts for example, as there are in the provisions for formalities for dispositions amongst the living. The statutes apply to outright gifts (legacies of personalty, devises of land) direct to the beneficiary, and to transfers made to trustees on trust for the beneficiaries.

But to state that no will may be valid unless it satisfies the statutory formalities, solves only half the problem. We first have to understand what a will is, before we can apply the rule. Plainly the test is not a formal one – it does not matter what the deceased called his will – he cannot avoid the operation of the law by calling his will a railway timetable, say. So the test is bound to be substantive. A disposition of property taking effect on death is a will, and it must be made in conformity with the formalities provisions. It must be seen at once that judges have not been willing to apply this provision rigorously, possibly because some arrangements which have this characteristic had grown up on a huge commercial scale before they had come up for adjudication under this head. So, some insurance and pension schemes under which provision is made by X so that on her death, payments are made to the last person she nominates, look like wills in analytical terms, but courts do not strike them down for failure to comply with the formalities. Likewise, where X opens a joint bank account in the name of herself and Y. Y has no contractual relationship with the bank, and the contract which X makes with the bank gives Y no power to withdraw money during X's lifetime. But the arrangement between X and the bank also states that when X dies, Y, if he survives, will be beneficially entitled to the balance. Such an arrangement has all the characteristics of a will. In particular it has the ambulatory, or walking, characteristic which is central to the notion of a will. X does not leave control behind her, but continues to have the last say, and Y may get nothing at all if X empties the account on the day of her death. This is plainly a will, and seen to be such, but it has been held to be outside the ambit of the formalities provisions, for overtly commercial reasons: *Young v. Sealey* (1949).

Outside these commercial contexts, courts have to be aware that the line between disposition during life and disposition on death may not be easy to draw. Plainly, if X makes a disposition to Y on trust for X for life, remainder to Z absolutely, that is not a will. Z takes an interest immediately the disposition is made to Y, even though enjoyment is postponed until X's death. Z's interest is vested in interest, though not in possession, during the life of X. Even if X reserves a power of revocation of the settlement, it is still not a will. Even if she goes so far as to give Y a power to apply capital to the life tenant (herself), we are still (just) making dispositions amongst the living. But what if, in addition, X becomes Y also, and makes herself trustee? She now has the life interest, the settlor's power of revocation and the trustee's power to apply capital to herself. The arrangement has become ambulatory and should attract the application of the formalities governing wills. The property is substantially passing on X's death, even though it is dressed up to look like an immediate defeasible living gift to Z.

The purpose of the rules outlined above in the case of a disposition taking effect on death via the medium of trustees is that the legal interest and the beneficial equitable interest should both be disposed of in compliance with the formalities. Courts have a reserve power which they occasionally bring out with devastating effect to provide that there should be no delegation of testamentary power. The trustee cannot name the beneficiaries. Plans for testamentary discretionary trusts, where the trustee not only selects amongst a class of beneficiaries, but also chooses who they are to be, look very vulnerable. The judicial power is not only not dead, but has recently made an appearance in the law of powers as 'the principle against non-delegation' and considered in the case of a disposition made even by a living settlor. This may be no more than the duty to act personally, discussed below at page 131. As we go to press, the Ontario Court of Appeal has supported delegation by validating a testamentary general power of appointment (*Re Nicholls*, 1987). But there are two situations where the courts have cooperated in devices which on the face of it looked like testamentary gifts without the statutory formalities.

FULLY SECRET TRUSTS AND THE PREVENTION OF FRAUD
The crudest situation arises where X is contemplating making a testamentary gift to Z. Y, who learns of the intention, prevails upon X not to make the gift to Z, but to leave it to him, Y, on the express understanding that Y will hold it on trust for Z. X, on the strength of this representation, makes a will leaving the property to Y. There is no mention of a trust on the face of the will. At the time of making this representation, Y intends, after X's death, fraudulently to conceal evidence of these negotiations and to hold the property beneficially for himself. A similar fact situation would be where Y was X's intestate successor and prevented X from making a will at all, by a similar story; but it is the first story which dominates the cases. Objectively speaking, both X and Y appear to intend that there should be a trust, but subjectively Y has other ideas. Y is guilty of fraud in the most basic sense. He is deceiving X and he intends to procure a profit from his deceit. We are not considering a case where

he later changes his mind, or finds he cannot perform: he is beguiling the testator from the outset.

But if we apply the testamentary formalities rules in a mechanical way, it is clear that he will keep his profit. If, however, we apply a functional or purposive interpretation of the formalities rules, we note that their principal purpose was to prevent fraud in the case of testamentary dispositions. If we now find the provisions being used to facilitate fraud, we have a problem which is not as instantly soluble as some think. If we go back to the efficiency criteria mentioned earlier, it may be better for the system to treat the attested document as the only admissible evidence of testamentary function and to refuse to use up judges' time on setting up what are in effect oral wills, to the detriment of other litigants waiting in line to have unavoidable disputes solved, and when the ultimate resolution of our case would inevitably be most costly in time. Against that we can set a public policy against villains, a sort of police function in the private law, drawing a line against unacceptably poor behaviour. And, of course, making it clear that fraud does not pay has its own efficiency factor in regulating people's behaviour out of court.

Taking the hard line is easier outside the courtroom than in it, and the judges have taken the personalised justice approach, at some cost in simple efficiency terms: the statute was to prevent fraud; here we find fraud being attempted by relying on the statutory provisions; we will not allow the statute to be used as an instrument of fraud, therefore we will allow other evidence than the unattested document to constitute the will. This line of reasoning clearly accepts that the disposition to Z is a testamentary disposition, and it is the formalities of testamentary disposition which the court is by-passing to prevent the fraud. There was another situation which gave rise to similar, if in a sense opposite, problems. Wills of land to the church were caught by the Mortmain legislation, which invalidated the gift on a public policy basis to protect the state interest (too much land coming into the hands of the church). One way round that was for X to leave land in her will to Y absolutely, on the strength of an undertaking by Y that he would apply it for the benefit of the church. Y's intentions here, in his relations with X, were wholly honourable and he intended to make the gift over during his lifetime, a disposition not caught by the mortmain statutes. The courts had no truck here with arguments about the arrangement being binding in morals only, and found a trust off the document, to which they applied the mortmain law. In this last case, on the basis of a fraud, in a loose sense, on the mortmain statute, the judges pushed the land back into the settlor's family, the invariable plaintiffs in these cases. In this example it is X and Y together who are joint villains. In such a case the court dare not leave the property with Y in case he acts honourably to X, and it turns the property back into the grateful hands of X's family. This reflects the law's normal approach to fraud – it undoes what the parties have already done and restores the parties to the status quo. 'Fraud unravels everything.' But in the first, non-mortmain, example, the judges took a momentous step and pushed the property forward to Z. This was probably the most sensible way to intervene against Y in this context, given that one function of a will is to defeat the intestate successor. If the property fell back into the estate, it was, in gambling terms, Grosvenor Square to a China orange that the heir would not pass it on to Z. So the device had two aspects worthy of note: first it by-passed a statutory provision which was clearly seen to be otherwise applicable, and secondly it made a theoretical contribution to the law of fraud by pushing the property forward to Z rather than letting it fall back to X's estate. It is in this configuration that we can talk of a doctrine, and the subject took on the name of Secret Trusts. There is no need for secrecy at all, of course, in the colloquial sense; it is quite possible for any number of people to know what Y has promised: the arrangement is secret in the sense that there is a will which is not revealed on the attested instrument, a hidden file that we may all know is there, but we cannot see.

If this were all, there would have been no insoluble legal or social difficulty with this doctrine. There was some overriding of statute, but it was friendly and purposive. There were clearly some problems about who might have to pay a legacy duty say, chargeable to the recipient, but ordinary trust doctrines of trustee and beneficiary seemed capable of dealing with them. There was some inefficiency, and time spent in courts investigating problems which of their nature were most intractable. In particular, since any evidence up to the date of death of the testator could be admitted, judges or the profession were bound to get involved in all sorts of loose and vaguely formulated conversations. Since the only act which the testator did to fix the beneficial interests was to die, and since he was unlikely to be able regularly to predict that, the evidence was bound to be in something of a mess. But villains were being stopped and Equity was back to the heady days of its youth, exercising an uncomplicated conscience jurisdiction. It must have been the case, on this basis, that if X on her deathbed had told Y that she had left him land absolutely but she wanted him now to agree that he would hold it on trust for Z, and Y had refused, leaving X no time to make alternative arrangements, then Y should have taken absolutely, there being no fraud and therefore no reason to by-pass the statute. Likewise the same kind of arrangement where Y agrees and honourably performs his agreement would not raise a secret trust but would be an arrangement of honour, operating outside the law. Again the recipient might only be intended to receive what Y took net of tax, though it might be an unfortunate consequence if Z had therefore to undergo a double tax deduction.

HALF-SECRET ARRANGEMENTS
But one development has caused the whole matter to be thrown into uncertainty. A testator, invariably one drawing up a will with legal advice, leaves property in her will 'to Y on trust' and tells Y, off the record, that it is intended to be held on trust for Z. Y acquiesces. Nothing can be the same if this arrangement is valid. Y cannot be committing fraud in the old sense, since he cannot benefit. X is plainly putting much less trust in Y here than she did above, a major qualification of the conscience aspect. Indeed Y's principal input into the scheme might have to be to say that the trust in favour of Z is indeed valid, since otherwise Y might look like Z's benefactor for tax purposes, which he may not want to do. If the arrangement is challenged, the dispute axis also changes. In the fully secret arrangement, the quarrel is between Y and Z; in this second case, it will be between X's estate and Z, since Y is on the face of the will excluded from benefit. If the arrangement does not work, Y will hold on trust for X's estate by operation of law as a bare trustee by what is known as a resulting trust. This resulting trust is not, of course, on the face of the will and would appear to be therefore a breach of the legislation, but appearances are deceptive: since the benefit is to X's estate, there is in fact no will of it – X cannot make a will in her own favour. And one might expect the death of Y before that of X to raise different policy issues in the two cases. It is nothing short of astonishing therefore to read academic opinion taking the view that

'the addition of two small words' to a secret trust should make no difference.

It should be observed that all the testators we have come across know how to make a valid will, since the legal estate to the trustee has always been correctly transferred. We have not either, in our calculations above, yet enquired whether X's motives for secrecy are worth taking into account in introducing this element of inefficiency into the law. But now we have a testamentary arrangement, drawn up by legal advisers ('on trust' is not a kitchen table expression) whereby the parties decide to give the statutory provisions the go-by. We now have to set quite different values against the imported inefficiency. People, usually men, may wish to leave property after their death to persons whose existence they wish, after death, to continue to hide from their families. This might not be thought to be an immediately attractive motive for a court of conscience, though it has to be said that if the 'secret people' would otherwise not become intended beneficiaries, that might be a factor. Bank accounts and insurance policies, however, which do the same trick, come close to satisfying most needs. But the House of Lords in *Blackwell v. Blackwell* (1929) put the seal of approval on the arrangement. The basis of this variety, the half- or semi-secret trust, is said to be the intention of X, the communication of that intention to Y, and Y's acquiescence in it. Even if it could be argued that fully secret trusts have no place in a section of a book dealing with intentionally created trusts, this case puts semi-secret trusts firmly into it. The new basis shows clearly that statute will be set aside simply because the parties want it – contract or conspiracy, according to taste. The statute is treated as a private law provision which private parties can take up or not as they so wish, rather than a public law provision with all sorts of public interest justifications. This case must be seen as a high watermark of the 'individualised justice' school of decision-making. The new juridical basis cannot have been meant to apply to fully secret trusts, since the House of Lords in *McCormick v. Grogan* in 1869 had decided that the jurisdiction to intervene was based entirely on personal fraud. Before 1966 the House of Lords did not have the power to alter a reason given by an earlier House as the basis of an assumption of jurisdiction. Outside the mortmain area, fraud did not just happen to be present, it was the very essence of the case. So after 1929 fully and half-secret trusts had different juridical bases.

OPERATION 'OUTSIDE THE WILL'

But even more unsettling was a slogan which *Blackwell* placed at the forefront of legal debate. Half-secret trusts, perhaps fully secret trusts, were said to operate 'outside the will'. This mystical expression is little explained. It sometimes appears even more mystifyingly translated into French (*dehors*) or into Latin (*aliunde*). If it means the trust is not mentioned in the attested document, it is not worth pausing over: that is the problem. The slogan is clearly designed to help us explain how it can be both off that document and still work. It is true, as we have seen, that the resulting trust to X's estate, if the device does not work, operates outside the will because in fact it effects no disposition, and it is in any event independent of any intention of X. But if Z takes a beneficial interest under the semi-secret trust, we have to ask when he gets it, and what he gets. If he gets a beneficial proprietary interest in the subject matter, and he gets it at the moment of X's death, neither before nor later, then he benefits from a disposition by X of property, taking effect substantially on X's death. He thus takes under a will made by X which is not in the form prescribed by statute. It should thus be void. If he takes before X's death, there is no problem, but on the cases so far, X would be surprised to learn that she had committed herself before death. If Z takes after X's death by way of trust, he must take by way of disposition from Y, which might surprise Y since the Revenue could then argue that there was a disposition to him by X and by him to Z, in which case two slices of tax might be due. The other possibility – that Z receives on X's death, not property, but only personal rights against Y – is worth exploration, but may not lead very far. If it were enough to eliminate will analysis, then any discretionary trusts, which also give their beneficiaries rights against the trustee, would also be outside the will – not a clearly desirable consequence. And even if all Z does take from X are rights only against Y rather than rights in the property which X was intending that Z should eventually take the benefit from, the rights against Y seem to be transmissible and to be themselves property, and should thus be disposed of in an attested document. It could be argued, however, that those rights against the trustee are not rights which the testator ever had, and so he cannot be disposing of them. 'Dispositions' in will definitions must, however, have a very wide meaning, otherwise equitable interests created in a will trust would not be dispositions either, since our testator never had them: plainly not the law. And if the legal estate is not correctly transferred to the trustee Y, because, for instance, it is insufficiently attested, what then? Does the gift to Z still take effect 'outside the will'? Sloganising in French or Latin is plainly no substitute for analysis, and the notion lacks convincing explanation. Half-secret trusts had in 1929 joined insurance and pension schemes, joint bank accounts and the like as will-substitutes but without the commercial constraint of a fear of unsettling many existing transactions.

CONTRACTION AND EXPANSION

Eight years later the Court of Appeal brought the new and rather unruly creature under some control by declaring that in a half-secret trust, intention, communication and acquiescence must all take place before the attested will or confirming codicil were executed. This at least forces X to focus on a particular arrangement and reduces the scope of the court's inquiry into what was the deceased's intention. Since we are no longer chasing common cheats, public policy might justifiably seek to promote efficiency and reduce individualised justice in this case. But in our own time, Brightman J in *Ottaway v. Norman* (1972) has opened the matter up. He decided that fully secret trusts need not be based on fraud and that communication could still be at any time up to death. Substantially informal oral wills are now possible in English law. I can visit a solicitor friend and tell him to draw up a will nominating himself as sole beneficiary. I can make plain to him what he will already know, that he is not intended to take beneficially but is intended to be a secret trustee, and we can agree that I will drop into the office from time to time and let him know who is to take the beneficial interests. I do not have to put anything else into writing and I am under no compulsion from the law to face up to putting my disordered intentions into a coordinated shape. When I die, my friend will have the job of putting it all together and may end up in court in an attempt to find an authoritative answer to his difficulties. *Cui bono*? (Latin, for 'To whom the benefit?')

SOME COMPLICATIONS

These difficulties are quite separate from those arising from the courts' attempts to work out the implications of secret trusts. A witness to a will may not take a benefit under the will. May a secret beneficiary who witnesses take such a benefit? If the function of the rule is to ensure that we have witnesses of testamentary capacity etc. who have nothing to gain or lose by their testimony, we should answer that he should not be permitted to take a benefit. It is no answer to say that he may not know at the time of attestation that he is a beneficiary, since on the one hand he may know, and on the other, beneficiaries taking on the face of the document, to whom the rule clearly applies, may not know either. Sloganising again will not solve an important policy issue, but it has been held without much consideration of policy that such a beneficiary takes. And what if a secret beneficiary, Z, predeceases X? How then can it be said both that Z takes and that the gift takes effect outside the will? Romer J in *Re Gardner, No. 2* (1923) saw the difficulty of the ambulatory nature of the will vehicle, and since Y was intestate successor, invented a declaration of trust by Y of whatever might come to him on intestacy from X, on trust for Z. This hardly solves the problem when Y is not intestate successor, and in any event should run into the severe problem that what reaches Y by intestate succession in this way is, at the moment of the declaration, future property and on principle the declaration of trust should be void for ever. Nor is it easy to see, if Y is also a life beneficiary of the secret trust, with power to dip into capital before Z comes along, how the subject matter satisfies the certainty rules. The notion of defeasible property mooted as a way of solving the *Livingston* case (1965) may be the simplest answer. The question also arises in some of these cases where no motive for secrecy seems to exist: why, if we give the scheme legal effect, did X insist on leaving it out of the will? Finally, what do we do with a bona fide purchaser of a legal estate who has given no value without notice of a secret trust? (Purchaser in this rule does not mean what it means in sale of goods, it means someone who takes by act of parties and not by mere operation of law.) Do we treat him just as if the trust was on the paper, as if the secret trust were indistinguishable from an institutional express private trust, and so make him choose between abjectly giving up when challenged by Z, or fighting on in the hope that Z will not be able to sustain his case at the end of his week in court? Is this the kind of choice it is the policy of the formalities provisions to force on the purchaser? The present answer of the courts is that it is: *Ottaway v. Norman* again, where an executor of a secret trustee failed in his attempt to set up his own adverse title as legatee under her will: a trust is a trust is a trust. We shall come back to this in the section on constructive trusts.

SECRET AND HALF-SECRET TRUSTS AMONGST THE LIVING?

Doubt also exists as to whether secret trusts apply to dispositions taking effect amongst the living. Authority is not clear. Cases where the beneficial interest falls back to X we may dismiss as being part of general fraud doctrine, as we may their extension of the notion of fraud to include later changing your mind. Except in freak cases where she dies prematurely, of course, there is not the same need here, since letting the property fall back to X will simply give her the chance to try again. A nineteenth-century court, reversing a judgment of Kekewich J (a task which, tradition cruelly has it, they might not have approached with due caution), has been taken as authority for the *inter vivos* application of the doctrine (*Rochefoucauld v. Bousted*, 1897). But in that case the court seems only to have seen itself as applying the ordinary fraud rule, and it gave back to the plaintiff property which had once belonged to her and which the defendant was said fraudulently to have acquired under a sale by mortgagees. If the doctrine does apply *inter vivos*, it should apply to dispositions of equitable interests so as to make them move forward, and all the settled law on section 53 of the Law of Property Act 1925 will be up for reconsideration. The fun to be had in the *Grey* area, if half-secret trusts are to be valid amongst the living, will be easy to imagine. *Grey* might itself be silent authority that it cannot be. If they do not apply amongst the living, we are spared the agonies of classifying them as express, constructive etc., since the formalities legislation on testamentary disposition treats all dispositions alike.

Secret trusts fascinate lawyers, in and out of the law schools, not because of their commercial importance or because they are believed to be so widely used or abused by the populace, but because they raise vital issues about the nature of adjudication and its relation to statute, and they heighten our understanding of the edges of judicial intervention. They form a topic on which we can easily sharpen our perceptions of the purposes of law and ask ourselves what are the limits of judicial adventurism. Having asked that, much is to be said for not stepping outside the narrow limits of *McCormick v. Grogan*.

4. DECLARATION OF TRUST

Our last basic proprietary mode is where the settlor, X, declares herself trustee of property in which she has a beneficial interest. It seems that whatever the nature of her beneficial interest, legal or equitable, if it is over land, she must declare in writing (Law of Property Act 1925, section 53(i)(b)). If she has a beneficial legal interest in personalty, she can make the declaration without formalities of any sort, by spoken words or any other form of communication; she is creating, not disposing. And despite a nineteenth-century attempt to parade Equity's prejudices against gratuitous acts, it has long been clear that she can do so by way of gift. She need give no notice to anyone, and if she does so secretly and in writing and then goes bankrupt shortly thereafter, she is likely to find herself put under close scrutiny by her creditors who will be looking to set the declaration aside for what is known as fraudulent preference, since property held by a bankrupt on trust is not available for the payment of her debts. But if she can show she was far enough away from the symptoms of bankruptcy, the declaration will be valid and effective to block the creditors. This is a formidable weapon. I can informally transfer to you my economic advantages in chattels of huge value by a few significantly chosen words, and once simply done the act cannot be revoked. No other device in this legal system approaches the massive power of these spoken words in Equity: 'I declare myself trustee of this for you.' If the subject matter of the declaration was an equitable interest, the complexities, predictably, gather. The case is one where Y holds on trust for X and X declares herself trustee of her equitable interest for Z. Must this be done in writing? If it operates as a true declaration, analysis and functionalism agree that it need not. As a true declaration, Y will continue to pay over income or capital to X and she will pay them over to Z. She does not need writing to tell herself what she has done, though her successors are again prejudiced. But there is some authority that in such a case, at least if X's only duties are to act as a conduit for assets distributed by Y, X drops out of the picture and Y is obliged to pay the money direct to Z. If we now take the formal position that since X declared herself trustee of personalty, there is no statutory provision requiring writing; an oral act, with all its inherent mischiefs for Y, will suffice. But if we take the view that the act, validated in this fashion, operates in effect by way of assignment and that in substance that is what it is, then we should, as the *Grey* court did, treat it as a disposition and require writing. The paper trail would then be established. Throughout all this debate of the function of the writing provisions, we have, however, been ignoring one weak link in the philosophy. The statute does not require our assignor or disponor to release the writing to anyone, and it is perhaps simply assumed that the assignee will have it. But at least if writing exists Y has a chance of seeing it in some context or another. If it does not exist, he is undoubtedly in a worse position.

A declaration of trust, being a property transaction, needs property on which to operate. If there is no property – because, for instance, the subject matter is future property, either property not yet in existence or property which although in existence is not yet owned by the declaror – then nothing has happened and the act is a nullity. This is subject to one major qualification, to which we now turn.

5. PROMISES OR AGREEMENTS TO PERFORM PROPRIETARY ACTS

RECHARACTERISATION

Common law and Equity are agreed that in some circumstances they will recharacterise a failed proprietary act as an agreement to perform the same act. So a judge may be faced with an agreement from two basic sets of facts. The first and cleanest example is where a party uses words of agreement – 'I agree to transfer, to declare myself' etc. The other is where the words used were words of grant, but where they are recharacterised into words of agreement because they fail as grants. It is clear that where words of grant fail for lack of formality, and where the purported grant is for value, then the words of grant will be read as words of agreement. Where a grant fails for substantive reasons, the issue is more complex. If the substantive defect is permanent, there is no point treating it as an agreement. To take an example from land law: a lease must, it is said, be of a fixed duration, or one capable of being fixed. So a lease granted under seal 'for the duration of the war' fails for a substantive reason. Treating it as an agreement to execute such a lease is futile because even if granted it will still be void, and the judges have not fallen into the trap. Where the defect is a lack of title in the grantor, the grantee may take some protection under the law of estoppel, and if the grantor subsequently acquires a title, the grant will be validated – the so-called feeding of the estoppel.

An assignment of property not yet in existence fails, not for formal, but for substantive reasons: assignment predisposes subject matter. But the defect is not permanent: the property may come into existence and it may come into the hands of the would-be transferor. Since words of agreement are capable of looking to the future, it is not futile to treat the assignment as a contract to assign and let it wait around for something to operate on. It is even reasonable to hold the 'assignor' liable for breach of contract if the property never comes into existence, if the other conditions of contractual liability, like consideration, are present. The cases are agreed that Equity will treat an assignment of future property as an agreement to assign it, if it is made for value. This is in keeping with Equity's limited kindness to would-be beneficiaries: it will only assist them if they have given value. To recharacterise is to assist, and so value is the precondition for recharacterisation. But it cannot be pretended that all Chancery judges have kept this principle in mind when looking at recharacterisation, and there have been occasions where the principles have been more broadly stated – that Equity always recharacterises failed assignments. These remarks are not supported by reasoned argument, and in any event, the damage done, if any, is so far minimal.

FORMALITIES

Agreements for the sale or other disposition of land are caught by section 40 of the Law of Property Act 1925. This introduces us to a most important concept, that of a valid but unenforceable contract. The statute imposes a formal requirement of written signed evidence of the contract, if an action is to be brought upon it. This requirement may be observed on one side only. So if A and B contract to sell land and B signs and A does not, A can sue B, but B cannot sue A. The contract is what is sometimes (not often) referred to as imperfectly synallagmatic. But the contract is still valid for both parties and if A performs any part of his contract by, for example, handing over a deposit, it is performance of the contract and may not be unravelled by any devices which allow parties to get back assets paid over without obligation. This notion of a valid but unenforceable contract may be a key to understanding some of the law in this area. It has to be said, though, that this analysis cannot be applied to transfers. A transfer is a present act without future reference. It cannot be enforced. It is either valid, in which case it works, or it fails. It cannot, as a transfer, hang around waiting for its subject matter.

Equity does not require writing for a valid and enforceable contract for the disposition of an interest in land. If the contract is specifically enforceable, which requires, amongst other things, that it must be made for value, and if there is a sufficient act of part performance of it, Equity will enforce it in the absence of writing. It will also recognise the common law writing formalities in lieu of part performance, but not in lieu of its requirements for specific performance.

There are no formal requirements for the sale or other disposition of legal interests in personalty.

AGREEMENTS FOR VALUE
An agreement for value will be enforced at law by an action for a money judgment. Unless there is some question of mistake, for example, it will not by itself be a defence that at the date the contract was made, the property which was its subject matter was not in existence or, though in existence, was not owned by the promisor. Were this not true, the commercial world would collapse tomorrow, and the commodities markets before that. An agreement for value has two different characteristics in Equity. In the first place the remedy is Specific Performance, and secondly value has a different meaning. Equity has not so far fallen into the common law trap of deciding that because it could not judge the adequacy of consideration, it could not distinguish a promise supported by sham consideration from a commercial bargain, albeit a poor one on one side: Equity does not recognise nominal consideration. On the other side, Equity will in one special context, that of a marriage settlement, recognise that the spouses and issue of the marriage have given

consideration, even though no commercial value has been given; they are said to be within the marriage consideration.

So if X promises Y for value to assign such property as she may receive under the will of her mother, who is still living, to Y, on trust for Z, she will be bound to transfer it, if and when her mother dies leaving her any property. At common law, if she does not do so, she will be liable in an action for a money judgment, and in Equity she will be liable to a decree of specific performance, requiring her to settle the property if she receives it. If the only property is money or even commercial fungibles, in principle only the damages action should lie, since Equity does not decree specific performance of contracts to pay sums of money or to transfer bags of corn (the common law remedy was quite adequate, so there was no basis for assuming jurisdiction). In this latter case, the rules as to the running of time on contractual claims apply, and so the action could become 'statute barred' under the limitation statutes. If the value came only from Y, the promisee, it ought also to follow both at law and in Equity that if Y decides not to proceed, that is up to him; but if value has been given by Z, then he can compel Y to enforce the promise. If they have both given value, either should be able to insist on enforcement.

So where X's promise for value to Y is to settle on trust for Z 'the Blackacre estate, presently owned by my Uncle Bill, if he leaves it to me in his will' and Uncle Bill does the decent thing and leaves it to her, she will at that time be bound to convey it to Y and a decree of specific performance will lie to enforce the conveyance. But 'Equity looks on that as done which ought to be done' and so she will be regarded in Equity as if she had made the conveyance as soon as she received it from Uncle Bill: she may retain the legal estate but she will hold it on trust for Z. Statutes barring contractual actions for lapse of time will not apply since X is now simply a trustee. This is certainly true if the value came from Z; it is less certain and certainly less obviously right if the value comes only from Y. But what if X's promise for value to Y is to settle 'whatever my Uncle Bill leaves me in his will' and Uncle Bill leaves her £10,000? The promise could have caught things of special value, but in fact produced only money. No specific performance will lie and so the 'looking as done' rule does not seem able to operate. Statute barring seems to be the risk for Z. What if now we know that X bought bonds with the money and gave them to A, who knew everything that we know? It has been held that A held the bonds on trust, because the money itself became bound by the trust the moment X received it, and that the money could be traced into the bonds (*Pullan v. Koe*, 1913). It is not clear that this works if you do it slowly: the deeming rule can only begin to operate after X receives her bequest, and specific performance does not at that moment lie. Furthermore, if Z's only claim to having given value is that he is a child beneficiary under a marriage settlement, he might also worry about whether Uncle Bill died before Z was born, if X decides not to perform. If X has disposed of the property before Z's birth, is it bound in the hands of a knowing transferee?

AGREEMENTS FOR VALUE AND DISPOSITIONS OF EQUITABLE INTERESTS

Say shares in a company are held by Y on trust for X for life, remainder to Z absolutely. In the ordinary course, therefore, X will receive any income produced by the shares during her life, and when she dies they will be held beneficially for Z alone. X, the life tenant, and Z now orally agree that in exchange for assets which X will transfer to Z, Z will transfer his future interest in the shares to X, so as to make her absolutely entitled in Equity. X, Y and Z then execute a deed of release marking the end of the old trusts and stating that the shares are now held by Y on trust for X absolutely. Y, the trustee, then transfers the shares to X in writing. The Revenue claim that this last written transfer attracted duty because it was a transfer of property on sale. X replies that the agreement for value to exchange the shares, under the 'looking on as done' rule, had the effect that Z at once, or at least when the value was paid over, held the future interest in the shares on trust for her, a constructive trust, and that it was thus the agreement which passed the property and not the written transfer. (Specific performance may be given of a contract to transfer shares.) Under the Law of Property Act 1925, section 53(2), constructive trusts are exempt from the writing requirements of section 53(i)(c) and so the transfer had taken effect without having to comply with the formalities section (*Oughtred v. IRC*, 1959). A bare majority of the House of Lords rejected this analytically highly seductive defence.

Functionally, of course, it would have been disastrous if there were to be no need for a paper trail on the assignment of an equitable interest for value. There is no legal necessity to involve the trustee in such a deal, and he would lose all his protection. The case seems to protect this point of view by a conclusion that the constructive trust raised by an agreement to assign for value does not pass all the equitable interest for the purposes of section 53(i)(c) and that some scintilla, or spark, of title remained in Z. That meant that the shares were still in a sense held by Y on trust for Z and any attempt by Z to dispose of that spark to X would attract the section 53(i)(c) requirement. Such a conclusion protects the functional requirement. But at the end of this story there was no trustee and that is the point at which *Oughtred* is most open to challenge. Whether the trustee, Y, conveyed the legal title in the shares to X because Z had told him to (exactly like *Vandervell*), or had done so at the request of X (Z being estopped from interfering by the constructive trust), or had simply acted on his own initiative and with the consent of X, relying on the deed of release, does not matter. There are no trusts remaining and no trustees to protect: there is no need for a paper trail and the final transfer was not in fact all it purported to be. It transferred the legal estate and it destroyed whatever residue or scintilla of equitable interest that section 53(i)(c) had kept in Z. No need for writing throughout: destruction not transfer. Perhaps the most important lesson, however, from *Oughtred* is the reminder that we should not expect a constructive trust to behave for all purposes like the institutional express private trust.

6. VOLUNTARY OR GRATUITOUS PROMISES

Voluntary promises are unilateral in a way in which agreements are not. The promisor is not asking the consent of the promisee and he is not getting anything in return for his promise. Voluntary promises are a controversial topic in Equity. They involve, though they do not always reveal, basic attitudes towards the limits of legal intervention (ism) in our society. In this respect they share some similarities with secret trusts; and the basis for the enforcement of promises made to dying persons would be an obvious link with that subject.

NECESSARY AND SUFFICIENT CONDITIONS AGAIN: SEALS
AND BARGAINS

The problem in a sense starts with the attitude of the common law.
That system operates two quite contrasting attitudes to the formation of promise or agreement liability. On the one hand it runs what
is historically the modern doctrine, taught as contract in all law
schools, that of bargain liability. It is not enough in this scheme to
intend seriously to engage in legal relations. If I promise you in the
most solemn circumstances imaginable, say, in the presence of the
Lord Chancellor, and fully intending to create a legal obligation,
that I will give you £100 on your birthday, I am under no liability.
My intention to be legally bound is a necessary condition for my
liability, but it is not sufficient. Nor is it enough that you agree to
accept it: to be enforceable at law, the promise or agreement must
form part of a bargain. If I do not now pay you, I will not be
regarded by our friends as a very nice person (unless, of course, by
the time your birthday comes round, I do not actually have £100 to
give you, in which case I do not even arouse moral opprobrium; or if
you are no longer being very nice to me). But the moral stigma which
attaches to me is not enough to generate legal liability. Common law
did not take over the church law breach of faith, though by accept-
ing nominal considerations it became a bargain theory which had
lost its way.

But long before all this was put together, the common law had
been enforcing promises made under seal. The chances are overwhelming that someone who writes and seals a promise intends it to
be binding, and it is not something you do easily by accident. But the
seal was not simply evidence of an intention to be bound: if the seal
fell off the document, so did the obligation. There was no point
proving it had once been sealed. And if I paid you in pursuance of a
sealed instrument and omitted to take it back or have it cancelled,
you could sue me again. Seals were, to steal the language of the
Scandinavian philosopher, Hagerström (and perhaps even a former
captain of Liverpool FC), magic. This was an ancient doctrine at
common law and the new law did not evict it. The common law continued with the two contrasting philosophies. If I promise you under
sealed writing that I will give you £100 on your birthday, you will

have an action at common law to enforce it. It may be important to say that if all you seek in your action is the £100, you are not suing me for damages caused by my breach, but for the performance of my obligation. You are suing on the contract, not for its breach. You cannot be met by any contractual damages defences about non-foreseeability, and you will not have to prove loss. If, however, you seek more than £100, you will, as to the excess, have to prove loss and you may be met by defences from the law of damages. This should also be just as true for a promise to give you a gold watch worth £100. This will be an important point to bear in mind later. These sealed promises are called covenants.

BARGAINS ONLY, IN EQUITY

Equity, however, as we saw, was a latecomer in our legal system. It was not required to obey the law of sealed instruments any more than any other formal rule of the early common law, and it embraced the new contractual philosophy with enthusiasm. If it was called upon to intervene in contractual matters, it would, as we saw above, do so only for bargains made for real value. Mock bargains, for nominal consideration, it would not strike down as unconscionable, and they remained valid at common law; but you could not get equitable help for them. You cannot obtain specific performance of my voluntary promise under seal to give you my Picasso drawing on your birthday. My intention to be bound does not matter in Equity, which is in this sense 'seal-blind'. You can, of course, sue me at law and you will get a judgment for at least the value of the drawing. The crunch, however, comes when Equity is necessarily drawn into the debate by the involvement of a trust.

VOLUNTARY COVENANTS WITH 'TRUSTEES'

What if X voluntarily covenants with Y, to give Y her Picasso drawing, or the Picasso drawing she hopes I will leave her in my will, *on trust* for Z. At no stage does the transaction operate at common law alone, giving Y any rights under the covenant, since the covenant is made to him as trustee, any more than would a simple transfer of property to Y on trust for Z give Y beneficial property rights at common law. The creator of the deal has invoked the Equity jurisdiction, and so the Equity rules apply. Those rules say they will not enforce covenants made without value: Y may not therefore constitute himself a trustee by litigation. It is no longer like a gratuitous dealing entirely at common law, where there was no invocation of jurisdiction and the common law was left to take its unassisted course. Y is told that if X will not pay, that is to be the end of the matter. You cannot sue for presents in Equity, or more grandly and more remotely, 'Equity will not assist a volunteer' (which in this expression means someone who has not given value or is not within a marriage consideration). So it was held in *Re Kay* (1939). This rule will not, however, apply to Z. If Z is party to a voluntary covenant by X that she will transfer property to Y on trust for Z, and she fails to do so, Z, as a party to the covenant, will be able to sue at law for enforcement. Z has undertaken no equitable obligations, nor does the promise purport to be made to him in any fiduciary capacity. Nor will the result be the same if A, a fourth party, who is also a covenantee of X's promise, whether or not he has given consideration for it, chooses to sue. If X declines to perform, A, who is not named as a trustee, may sue at law to enforce the covenant. And it matters whether or not Y can himself sue, because if he can he will recover the value of performance of the covenant quite independently of questions about whether he can recover damages caused by late performance. What is also clear is that if he can recover damages, they should in principle be based on the expectations and loss of Z and not those of Y. Nor does anything in *Re Kay* deny the proposition that a trustee of an existing trust might contract as trustee with third parties, and enforce the contract, even if it were voluntary. Here the trustee-beneficiary relationship already exists and the court does not deprive beneficiaries of benefits, contracted for on their behalf by the trustee. No assistance is needed to create a trust relationship, though of course the trustee would in the case of a voluntary covenant have to make do with common law remedies. It cannot be pretended however that the law allowing existing trustees to sue on voluntary covenants does not constitute a somewhat artificial distinction with *Re Kay*. It is the foundation of much charitable fund-raising.

VALID BUT UNENFORCEABLE VOLUNTARY COVENANTS IN EQUITY

That is not, however, the end of the matter. Two further questions have to be considered. First, it seems that covenants made without consideration are not void in Equity, as assignments of future property are. They appear to be valid but unenforceable. So if X, our voluntary covenantor, in fact delivers the property to Y, a trust will in the normal way be irrevocably constituted for the benefit of Z. X cannot recall it on the basis that it was paid out under a void transaction. This indeed may reveal one of the principal family functions of voluntary covenants. The covenant will often be under seal as part of a wider arrangement, settling other property, or as part of a scheme of family arrangement. The seal will therefore often be merely incidental, being present on a larger document of which the covenant is a part, in order to pass legal interests in land. When the property then falls in, by the happening of a future event, there is no need to execute a separate document, repeating the trusts set out in the main transaction; a simple transfer to the trustees will see to it that the future property is held on the trusts of the main settlement, without further complication. Though it is a trap to ask why people do things if they do not wish to be legally bound (as if, by so asking, we are abandoning our right to determine the kinds of issue we want to see litigated in our courts, by letting them make that decision for us), there is a perfectly good socio-legal explanation of voluntary covenants in this pattern of behaviour.

INVOLUNTARY DELIVERY

The covenant seems able to stay in existence, though, with a more extended range of effect. It seems that if the property reaches Y in a manner not foreseen by X, and not by her hand, the covenant may operate to prevent her suing Y to recover it, and the trust may thus be indirectly constituted. So in *Re Ralli* (1964) where Y later became executor of a will under which future property, the subject matter of X's covenant to Y on trust for Z, was bequeathed to X, it was held that the trust was now constituted in the hands of Y on trust for Z. The limits of this rule are a little obscure. It was argued by analogy from *Strong v. Bird*, but it is more complex. In this kind of case, the executor Y has loyalties to two different individuals: X under the will and Z under the covenant. In the case in hand, Y opted for Z, but we are not told on what basis he did so, nor is it clear what remedy, if any, would lie to Z if Y had handed over the property to X. Nor is it obvious that he could have resisted an action by X if the property descending by will came by virtue of a contractual obligation generated in the testator's lifetime between the testator and X. The judge seemed to think also that the scenario only played out in this way if Y were made executor under the will. Following an earlier thought, we could ask what the result would be if Z were the executor. On this reasoning he might be free to deliver, not to his testator's legatee, X, but to Y, thereby constituting the trust.

Finally on this point, if what was said above about recharacterisation of failed grants as promises is correct, a voluntary assignment, even under seal, of future property will not be recharacterised as a covenant to convey. It is at this point that that issue begins to have practical consequences. If the voluntary assignment *is* recharacterised as a voluntary covenant, under *Kay*, it will still not be enforced and so the recharacterisation has no effect. But if it is so recharacterised, and the property in fact reaches the hands of Y, the trust will be irrevocably constituted and Z will be home and dry. If, however, a voluntary assignment even under seal is void and not recharacterised, if the property gets into the hands of Y, even at the hands of X (or under a power of attorney whereby X gives Y power to collect it), it ought to be recoverable by X.

And we might ask how the rules would apply to voluntary covenants by X to declare herself trustee? If the property presently exists, it ought not to be bound since that would destroy the distinction between a declaration and a promise to declare. Even more so, then, if it is future property, it should not bind X when she receives it. The distinction between 'void' and 'valid but unenforceable' looks harder to maintain when the performance of the promise is in a sense 'to' the promisor.

TRUSTS OF CHOSES IN ACTION SPECIALLY CREATED FOR THE EVENT

The last point to watch is a variant of the conjurer's catchphrase: 'Now you don't see it, now you do.' A voluntary covenant lacks force because there is no consideration. A voluntary, fully constituted trust, however, like a completed gift at common law, is valid and irrevocable. So, two possibilities: first, what if there is in fact property being settled, but we cannot at first sight spot it; and secondly, if some people are engaging in such complex devices, why do we not recharacterise all voluntary covenants to make them take effect in this way, whether it is what the parties intend or not? The second is the easier question. Since the parties are volunteers, if what is done fails, principle and authority alike combine to say they are not to be assisted. Recharacterisation in these circumstances is no more than a cowardly way of abandoning the rule that Equity will not assist. And since the trick, as we shall see, would depend on the existence of a sealed document, and not work for all other sorts of seriously intended promises not under seal, Equity would at the same time be abandoning its long-held view that it looks at substance, not form. Voluntary covenantees have no more claim to our assistance than voluntary oral or written promisees who are seriously intended to be benefited.

The device to be looked at takes its origin in a rather confused nineteenth-century case, *Fletcher v. Fletcher* (1844). Here X, in a deed which he executed himself only, and kept quite secret, covenanted with Y that he would pay £60,000 to Y on trust for Z. After X's death Y discovered the deed and declined to act in the trusts unless so ordered by the court. Z brought an action to force Y to take steps to recover the £60,000 from X's executors. Z won, and the judge avoided the rule about not assisting a volunteer by stating that he was not doing so, since he was only giving the deed its common law effect. Not true, of course, since at common law the deed gave rights to Y to exercise for his own benefit and at his own choice; this judgment imposes an equitable duty on him to sue, but does not explain where it comes from. At this level, the case and much said in it are simply inconsistent with the decision of *Re Kay*, and must be regarded as contrary to principle. Another thread of reasoning in the case, however, justifies itself on the basis of the device we are now to consider, the trust of a covenant, or as it is now more widely known, the trust of a chose in action. The case itself does not bear serious analysis on this ground either, since the court does not keep separate the covenant and its proceeds, of which a trust could plainly be declared, but the idea as developed in modern times does. The question amounts to asking whether a valid trust is created if X comes up with something as follows: 'I voluntarily covenant with Y that I will pay Y the sum of £60, and I hereby vest the chose in action which represents the benefit of that covenant in Y on trust for Z.' The attempt is to produce a chose in action, a property right with a common law existence, to sue X for £60, and to vest that in Y, so constituting a voluntary but irrevocable trust.

The covenant is now only a precondition, a means of creating property, the chose in action, which itself is the subject matter of the trust, and that chose in action is safely at home with Y. No one would seek to enforce the covenant in Equity; there would have been a valid transfer. The only enforcement would be at law, where Y would enforce the covenant which he did not take as trustee.

The first doubt is on this last point. As in the secret trust debate, we have to ask ourselves whether we are in the real world here. If there is no measurable instant when Y has a beneficial right to enforce the covenant, then just like a transferee of physical property on trust, he takes it as trustee and is therefore under Equity's whip. Since the covenant is voluntary and he is inside the jurisdiction, *Re Kay* might be thought to say he cannot enforce, and so there exists no chose in action to make the subject matter of the trust. If there is a measurable moment when he has a beneficial interest, the trusts must be declared by Y, not by X, and this may have undesirable consequences for the parties in tax law. (This is not to question that Equity will not invalidate voluntary covenants taking effect wholly at law – if X owes me £10 under a voluntary covenant validly created at law, I can assign the benefit of that covenant, that chose in action, to you on trust for Z.) So, if Equity is seal-blind, and the whole operation takes place in Equity, it seems doomed; if it begins life at common law, and then moves into Equity, it may work, but not necessarily with the public law consequences which the parties would desire.

A last difficulty lies in recent developments in the law of choses in action. There was a view, which must now perhaps be called old-fashioned, that a promise to transfer future property did not create a chose in action, and could not therefore create a property right: choses in action were created only where the subject matter of the covenant was a debt presently due, or something like it. One judge even declined to pursue the recharacterisation exercise on the perfectly defensible view that since the property, subject matter of the covenant, was not, at the time of covenanting, the property of the covenantor, there was no point recharacterising since even if that were done, there would be no chose. This rather traditional restriction of the nature of choses in action may no longer be defensible, and they have on recent examination been shown to cover a wide range of contractual undertakings. It might be noted here, to reinforce the point made earlier about the confusion in *Fletcher v. Fletcher*, that no one thought to ask whether the covenantor in that case had £60,000 in the bank when he made the covenant. But then money may not be capable of being future property for the purposes of this rule. . . .

The substantive issue here of course is whether we want to enforce voluntary covenants in courts of law. Much of the clamour that we should is based on little more, in some cases, than the feeling that it is immoral to break solemn promises if intended to create legal relations. We have to decide whether we want to clutter up our courts with people suing for presents and whether indeed it is not somewhat ungracious behaviour on the part of such plaintiffs. Much law has been built around the covenant at common law and to abolish it now would be foolish, but it is far from clear that it would be foolish for Equity, which still has the choice, to extend the range. Given the narrowness of the point, it is not a matter of great import, but even when considering little steps, we have to ask whether they are in the right direction.

8

Trustees of Such Trusts

1. FIDUCIARY MANAGEMENT UNDER THE COURT

The trustees stand at the centre of the trust pentad of settlor, objects/beneficiaries, trustees, 'third' parties and the court. In the case of charitable trusts, the Crown, through the Attorney-General, makes up a hexad. An examination of their role is essential to understanding the nature of the trust. In the simplest case, the trustee will hold a legal estate on trust for the beneficiaries in Equity, but he may, under a sub-trust, hold an equitable interest as a trust estate on trust. A trustee may also be a settlor, and also a beneficiary, and all the beneficiaries of a trust can also be its trustees and its settlors (e.g. houses in shared ownership), though a sole beneficiary of a trust cannot also be sole trustee. The paradigm trustee in the old cases was a family friend, undertaking onerous duties as an act of great personal kindness. Such trustees still exist, but the modern law is dominated by the figure of the paid trustee – unit trust or pension fund manager, solicitor, trust corporation, public or private – who demands a different treatment, and some tension is created as lawyers attempt to twist the old law into a vehicle suitable for handling this latter group.

The trustee is fiduciary manager for the beneficiaries, on terms set either by the general law (triggered by the finding of a trust) or specially by the settlor. There may be some kind of consensual relationship between settlor and trustees, but enforcement is by the beneficiaries only: the terms of the trust are enforced by strangers to the transaction of creation, by virtue either of their equitable proprietary interest in the subject matter of the trust, or simply because the trust device gives them direct rights against the trustees, based on status, without giving them rights in the subject matter. (The suggestion made earlier that in 'abstract' purpose trusts, the settlor should become the enforcement agency, has to be made simply because no beneficiaries exist, but undoubtedly it would establish a new model of trust, close to simple contract.) And to the extent that the trustee wins in disputes about the administration of the trust, he does so against these beneficiaries. The settlor maintains a continuing influence only by virtue of any special terms he writes into his trust, such as a right to revoke the trust, or a power to appoint new trustees. The court makes up the pentad because in the law of trusts, Chancery judges have been more openly interventionist than their common law commercial brethren. Throughout the history of the trust the judges have been closely involved in many issues of administration and their role is integrated into its structure. The judges will themselves, if necessary, execute the trust, and the trustee's private law application to the court for directions has no common law counterpart.

Trusteeship, like marriage, would appear to be a private law status. Just as when one marries, one acquires a new legal status, acquired by consent, but some of its terms not necessarily known to, nor therefore agreed to, and certainly not variable by, the parties, so does the court's control of the notion of the trust fix powers and duties on trustees which they may never have dreamt of. Most importantly, a trustee may be removed from this status by order of the court. The beneficiaries are not restricted to waiting for something to go wrong, incurring loss and then suing for an account; they can divorce a trustee.

TRUSTEE NOT AN OWNER
Trusteeship is a bundle of legal relations, principally duties, powers, immunities, liabilities. It may also involve rights, but of a very limited kind. At the inception of the trust, on day one, the trustee has no enforceable rights against the trust property, since he cannot exercise any choice for his own benefit. The trust instrument may, however, give him rights to remuneration for work subsequently done in the administration of the trust, and he may also subsequently acquire rights to contribution and indemnity both from his fellow trustees and from the beneficiaries. This lack of initial rights makes it misleading to describe the trustee as an 'owner' of the trust assets, and creative thinking about the reform of trustee law, which

takes as its starting point a notion of what an owner should be able to do, will be likely to lead to inconsistent, not to say mischievous, results. The common law ownership of the trustee has been asset-stripped by Equity.

2. DUTIES

(a) Substantive duties

The trustee is dominated by his duties. Trustees' duties are divisible primarily into those which bind all trustees and those which only operate when special provision is made in the settlement constituting the trust. Such would be, for example, the duty to sell in a trust for sale. What follows, however, is an account of those duties which are common to all trustees. There are three substantive duties:

(i) To 'get in', or secure, the trust assets.

The trustee must take steps to assume control of the trust property and to reduce into possession such things as debts belonging to the trust.

(ii) To safeguard the trust assets and their value.

The trustee must invest the trust corpus in authorised investments. He may not let it lie unproductive. In the absence of express investment powers, different jurisdictions have taken different views as to how investments should be authorised. These differences appear to reflect fundamental attitudes towards the notion of trusteeship, or perhaps a perception of the content and prevalence of express investment powers, rather than differing economic conditions. Perhaps the oddest feature of this duty today in England and Wales is that trustees who buy land with trust money are – unless they have been given by the trust instrument a special power to do so, or are specially so authorised by statute – in breach of trust: land is not investment.

In England and Wales, for instance, statute in the shape of the Trustee Investments Act 1961 has provided a 'legal list' system of some complexity with three classes of authorised investment in which the trustee must invest. Other jurisdictions have adopted a simple rule centred on 'prudence' as the governing factor, and the

English rule has some such overlay operating within its legal list. This approach says that investments must be made as they would be by the prudent man of business or the prudent trustee, with some variety of controlling rider that he is not to invest as he would on his own behalf, but as he would on behalf of others for whom he felt a moral obligation, avoiding speculation and maintaining a regard for the balance between capital and income. This latter aspect, which recognises that there are not only present beneficiaries in most trusts, but also holders of future interests waiting in the wings, and that the two groups will to some extent have competing interests, the first group wishing to maximise income and the latter group, capital growth, has formed the basis of separate subsidiary rules where there are assets of a wasting nature (which favour those presently entitled) or of a reversionary nature (which favour those entitled in the future). The effect of these rules is to require the trustees to hold an even hand between different classes of beneficiary.

(iii) To ensure that the benefits of the trust are distributed to the beneficiaries.
Capital must be distributed to those entitled to it, and so must income, unless the trustees have a power to convert income into capital, a so-called power to accumulate.

(b) Operational duties

Trustees have a further five duties governing the modality of the execution of the trust. They may perhaps all be summed up as the duty to act honourably, a notion which seems to combine elements of honesty and diligence.

(iv) To act honestly.
This is clearly the minimum duty of a fiduciary: the duty of good faith. It is a duty which we are all deemed capable of performing: it does not depend on intelligence or experience, and the unpaid family friend and the mighty trust corporation can perform it alike. It is hard to define what good faith amounts to, particularly since much of its detailed application is provided for in other rules below, but it amounts to more than absence of bad faith.

(v) To act with care.

This duty lies at a pivotal point on debates about the nature of trusteeship. As late as one hundred years ago, there was some authority that all a trustee had to do was his honest best: the duty of care was subjectivised, so that whatever any individual was capable of, that was what was due. It is, arguably, dishonourable to expect more. Settlors will appoint as trustees people whose characters or judgments they trust, but these persons may not have any real business acumen and, more importantly, may not even know that they do not have it. This subjective standard does not penalise the 'family friend' trustee, and is capable of being fairly applied to all kinds of trustee. It was rejected, however, in England, and has few friends elsewhere, partly on the grounds that it would lead to different standards being applied to different trustees within the same trust. This is not as convincing as it might be: if I trust myself to a team of doctors and nurses in a hospital, I expect different members of the team to live up to different standards of care.

It is a commonplace of trusts textbooks to state that a trustee is strictly liable for the performance of his duties and/or that he must exercise the utmost diligence (? a lower standard) in performing them. In exercising his powers, however, it is said that a lower standard is expected, that of the man of ordinary prudence in the management of his own affairs. If this is different from the standard expected in performing the investment function (that of the prudent man of business), it means that there are three, or perhaps four, standards of care to be considered. Modern authority for this strict liability for duties is scant if not non-existent (and some judicial observations fly in its face: 'It is the duty of a trustee to conduct the business of the trust with the same care as an ordinary prudent man of business . . .' *per* Brightman J in *Bartlett v. Barclays Bank*, 1980), nor should we accept that it is desirable or consonant with principle. It would purport to make a trustee virtually an insurer with respect to the performance of his duties, and mean that he could not defend an action for breach of duty by showing that he had exercised all ordinary care, since that would only be a defence to an action based on faulty exercise of a power.

For a number of reasons, establishing the strict duty liability may be hard. As we shall see, on the one hand, trustees are given powers which may to a large extent excuse them from the performance of their duties, and very often only the exercise of the power is challenged. On the other hand, many breach cases come before the court when an honest and reasonable trustee asks the court, under a statutory provision, to excuse him from any breach of trust he has committed or may have committed. The court does not have to make a finding of breach in order to give clearance; it can say, 'If there was a breach, we excuse it.' So we are deprived of a main source of clear examples of breach of trust by a trustee acting honestly and reasonably. Finally, the debate may centre around the so-called 'technical' breach of trust, which does not involve negligent conduct in the colloquial sense on the part of trustees, but even this may be no more than a deliberate breach committed under a mistake of law, which, as we all know, excuses no man. There seems no good reason or authority for this diversity of standard and quite possibly in practice trustees regard themselves as bound by the 'powers' standard of care, revolving around the notion of ordinary prudence, modified for the case of investment, perhaps, to take account of the business-like nature of the activity.

This standard is the minimum standard to be applied to all trustees. It is an objective standard, and is of course quite unfair to those trustees who do not possess ordinary prudence. But there is also authority that superimposed on this basic layer are one or more higher burdens. Paid trustees, such as solicitors or accountants, are said to be under a higher duty, though it is not clear whether this is objective or individuated: does the firm which charges £200 an hour have a higher burden than the firm that charges £40? Higher still, and seemingly with an individuated duty, are those professional trustees such as banks. They will, it seems, be bound to live up to the high standards which they hold themselves out as having; a subjective test, and higher than the objective test.

(vi) To derive no profit from the trust.
This is sometimes said to be a duty not to put oneself in a position where one's interest and one's duty conflict. These could be two formulations of the same rule or two slightly different rules. The difference would be revealed if a beneficiary complained that a trustee had put himself in a position where there was a duty/interest conflict, but where no profit had yet been made, and sought to have the trustee removed for this breach of trust.

The cases all involve situations where a profit has in fact been made, and the question has been whether it has been procured in breach of trust. The fact situations range from acquisitions of trust property, or some notional extension of it (like a renewal of a lease), which are voidable at the instance of the beneficiary, to the clawing back for the trust of remuneration received by the trustee by virtue of his office, and not authorised by the trust. These cases turn around the proposition that a trustee may obviously obtain remunerative employment while he is a trustee, but not as a trustee. The rule even extends to the acquisition of 'moral' benefits by trustees. A trustee who has entered into a morally but not legally binding contract to sell trust land and who receives a better offer, has a duty to probe that offer. He cannot do the commercially decent thing and proceed with his first purchaser to the possible loss of his beneficiaries. Such a course is not truly moral; the loss is not that of the trustee, and in these circumstances his appeal to morality is merely self-indulgence.

The general rule has recently received much criticism as being too harsh on trustees, and also on other fiduciaries (a sort of second-rank trustee whom we shall consider later in the section on constructive trusts) to whom it applies in modified form, and judges have been willing to soften its hard effects by permitting trustees to buy trust property under tightly drawn conditions. The issue is whether it is better for the greater good to let trustees know, for instance, that they should never buy trust property, because of the danger of undetectable overreaching, and cause trustees to look elsewhere for their investments; or to do justice on a more individual basis, but at the cost of greater uncertainty, and the sure knowledge that trustees, who hold all the best cards in such a contest, will occasionally be able to pull a fast one. All that is certain is that patronising remarks about how our predecessors had to have such rules because they could not be sure of getting to the bottom of the matter, whereas we, with our superior techniques, can do so, must be wide of the mark. As the judges' techniques develop, those of villains will do so at much the same rate.

It should be noted that trustees can always acquire trust property, and may be remunerated if so authorised, by the trust itself, and are always able to make agreements with the beneficiaries securing such benefits even if the trust instrument is silent. The court will also increase remuneration where it is thought to be beneficial for the administration of the trust. And rather oddly, solicitor trustees may keep their profit costs arising from litigation on behalf of the trust.

(vii) To keep accounts and records and provide information.
This duty would appear to be a necessary back-up to allow the beneficiaries to enforce all the preceding duties. It will also be useful to beneficiaries watching the exercise of powers by their trustees. But in England and many other jurisdictions, trustees are under no obligation, in the absence of bad faith – which cannot lightly be alleged – to give reasons or motives for the particular exercise of a power. This is a style of managerial control which has a certain old-fashioned attraction, and some people are clearly willing to exercise authority only if they do not have to give their reasons for doing so. It also seems better suited to the family friend trustee than the professional. In New Zealand and in some jurisdictions in Australia, legislation has imposed an obligation on trustees to give their reasons if so required by a judge, a compromise reform which seems not to have had corrosive effects on the fabric of society in those jurisdictions. Even in the UK we seem to have survived the innovation of judges always having to give their reasons.

(viii) To act personally.
This was the historical starting point of trusts law. The trustee either acted himself or handed over the trust to the administration of the Chancery. By the end of the nineteenth century, this highly incon-venient and expensive rule had been modified so that in certain cases, said to be of moral or legal necessity, the trustee could employ agents to do administrative acts. This duty is seriously affected by the statutory power to employ agents, discussed below.

These duties are general duties, imposed on all trustees by the courts. Individual trusts may in addition contain further duties. Trustees must perform these duties. Their powers, on the other hand, are said to be discretionary. What this means, and how their powers affect their duties, must now be considered.

3. POWERS

Trustees have two kinds of power, administrative and dispositive. Some of these powers are conferred by statute on all trustees (usually unless excluded by the settlor), and trust instruments will normally confer other powers on the trustees, to make their trusts workable. It would appear that Equity did not confer powers on trustees (subject to what is said above about powers of delegation) and that they thus have no inherent powers: if the statutes were repealed and no powers were expressly conferred by his settlor, a trustee would only have his duties, making the trust a virtual non-starter as a management device. Conversely, statute has largely avoided setting out duties. The Trustee Act 1925 has no section imposing duties on trustees, but it is dominated by the sections which confer powers on them. This decision to omit a statement of duties in the statute may be defended on the policy ground that it discourages the presentation of purely technical defences which statutory definitions so often encourage. The powers, on the other hand, may have to be strictly construed. The disadvantage with the Act's scheme is that it has not forced it to lay down principles on how to relate a trustee's duties to his powers. This is important because it is misleading to say that trustees are given powers to enable them to carry out their duties: some powers are conferred to allow trustees not to perform their duties. So a trustee may have a duty to do an act and a power not to do it. Relating those two notions is a subtle exercise, and since the powers are necessarily fiduciary powers exercisable for the benefit of others, parasitical (new) duties have to be attached to them.

The Trustee Act is now over half a century old and its list of powers looks a little threadbare for modern conditions. A trust which contains no express powers of its own and which relies only on the statutory powers is a poor-looking thing, and indeed some litigation indicates that the scheme established by the precedents and the statutes sometimes has the function of an obstacle course through which the prescient settlor must plot a safe route. The dangers of a single-sentence oral trust are more than merely evidential. Statutes in some Australian jurisdictions, in New Zealand and the United States, have reduced the risks by conferring a wider range of powers where the trust is silent. In an admirable report, perhaps the best modern survey of trusteeship, the *Ontario Law Reform Commission*

(1984) has urged its own legislature to follow suit. In the brief survey which follows we will look first at the powers conferred by the Trustee Act 1925 and then note the more recent additions in these other jurisdictions. Powers additionally conferred by settlors are not listed.

(a) Statutory administrative powers: England and Wales

The administrative powers of trustees conferred by statute include the following:

(i) Investment powers
It is rather odd to talk of a power to select investments since this would be a power which a trustee must exercise, but the phrase does express the obvious truth that someone has to interpret and apply the investment duty. The selection of investments is increasingly a problem for trustees. Many trusts are no longer family arrangements designed simply to maximise wealth, but may be set up by groups of people holding common political or ecological beliefs. Recent authority has emphasized that the trustees may not reflect their own personal or political beliefs to the prejudice of the trust investment, but it is not so obvious how far they may reflect the common interests of the beneficiaries – by not investing, for example, in companies operating in disapproved-of states or industries, without first obtaining consent of all their beneficiaries.

The powers given in the legislation effectively help to amplify the definition of trustee investments, by construing express investment powers, and they also confer powers supplementary to existing powers of investment. In addition they excuse what would otherwise be a breach of the duty to invest, by providing that a trustee will not be liable for continuing to hold investments which have ceased to be authorised 'only' by virtue of continuing so to hold them.

(ii) Power to compound liabilities
This is another 'defeating' power. It gives trustees wide discretion in their task of getting in the trust assets, and it allows them to proceed in such a way as not to get them in, by compromising or compounding with debtors, going so far even as allowing them to 'abandon' any such property. Such a power is plainly necessary if trustees are not to

waste trust assets chasing every bad debt, but it may, if exercised, have the effect of negating a principal duty. The Act says the trustees must exercise this power in good faith, and judicial interpretation has sensibly invented a duty on the trustees actively to consider the exercise of this power. A trustee who has done nothing cannot be heard to say, when assets have been lost, that he has abandoned assets under this statutory exemption.

(iii) Power to employ agents

This power, conferred by section 23, allows trustees to employ and pay an agent to do any act required to be done in the execution of the trust. It appears designed only to allow delegation of executive acts, and not discretions, but it does leave the duty to act personally much eroded. There must presumably be some positive act of delegation. The Act says that the trustee will not be liable for the default of the agent if employed in good faith. This is probably a reference to vicarious liability, that is, where only the agent is at fault. What is lacking in the statute is a clear statement that a trustee who defeats his duty to act personally by employing an agent, thereby assumes a revised primary operational duty, replacing his duty to act personally, namely a duty to supervise the agent. This is one of the clearest areas where the Act's failure to relate paired powers and duties has caused confusion. Trustees may also by power of attorney (a document under seal creating an agency) for a period of not more than one year delegate the whole of their duties under the trust, but remaining liable for all breaches committed by the donee of the power in that period.

(iv) Power to deposit money in a bank

This is a power to deposit money in a bank pending investment. It does not give trustees the power to keep money in a bank to pay day-to-day running expenses.

(v) Power to give receipts

This power, which was usually inserted in settlements which gave trustees either a duty or a power to sell land in order to achieve a specific purpose with the purchase money (paying off mortgages on other land, for example), allowed purchasers to escape the effects of the rather curious rule that such land, even when lawfully sold by trustees, remained fixed with its trust status until those purposes were achieved. There was authority that such express powers were not needed, at least in trusts for sale (where there is a duty to sell), and also that the power to give receipts discharging the purchaser from seeing that the purchase price was properly applied was incidental to the duty or power to sell; and this seems more consistent with principle. It should not be the business of lawful purchasers to take on the role of surrogate trustees. The statutory power settles the matter for all practical purposes, but leaves the theory looking rather untidy. Normally this power will be exercised by an agent under the delegation power. The power will not, of course, avail a purchaser who has knowledge that the sale is in breach of trust, and he will be bound by the trusts, receipt or no.

(vi) Power to insure
Even more startling, it is believed that a trustee has no duty to insure, and that if he does, he may only do so for three quarters of the value of the property, and that this power does not extend to bare trustees holding absolutely for any person who could demand a transfer of the property. Beneficiaries may of course insure their own equitable interest, but in many cases this will not be a sensible arrangement. Trustees holding a building under an express power to do so, on trust for infant beneficiaries, are apparently under no liability to them if they do not insure it and it is destroyed by fire. The duty to preserve and safeguard the trust assets must be performed by trustees sleeping on the premises, with a bucket of water by their side, and it is enough if they have done so . . .? Express powers/duties save the law from disgrace.

(vii) Power to concur with others
Trustees of one undivided share in property may, when exercising their role as trustees of that share, go into partnership, as it were, with the people who have rights over the other shares, even though the trustees may be beneficially entitled to one of those other shares. This power both increases the dealing potential of the property and absolves the trustee from the charge of putting himself in a duty/interest conflict.

(viii) Power of sale
Statute has not in England and Wales, though it has elsewhere, conferred general powers of sale of land on trustees. It has, however,

135

imposed duties to sell in some cases, for example where land is the subject of co-ownership. But it has conferred a limited power to sell chattels and also conferred additional powers for the sale of land where the settlement itself confers expressly or by implication a power or duty to sell. Power to postpone a sale has also been conferred on trustees who have a duty to sell in a trust for sale, thereby suspending the duty. The *Ontario Law Reform Commission Report* recommended a statutory power to sell, including a power to sell on credit. Sales incidental to investment policy are authorised by the duty to invest.

TRUSTEES' CONTRACTING POWERS: THE NON-CORPORATE TRUST

Trustees exercising powers of sale are in a curious position. Because they are contracting as trustees, they must seek the best price and may not yield to the demands of commercial morality by declining better offers, if they are still legally free to consider them: they cannot enhance their status at the club at the expense of their beneficiaries. On the other hand, since the trust is not a corporate entity, they contract in their own names and assume personal responsibility for their contracts. This is a useful curb on potential trustee enthusiasm for spending other people's money. But it can have damaging effects. In the case of a large trust, particularly commercial trusts, the amounts of money involved may easily exceed the sort of money which a trustee could produce from his own personal resources. The trustees will themselves be entitled to an indemnity from the trust, but for various reasons this may be for less than the amount of the debt. This will be particularly acute if the transaction is not one of sale, but of loan, which we will consider shortly. The net result is that outsiders may be less willing to deal with the trust. Recent suggestions for curing this defect have included the suggestion that it should be lawful for settlors to give their trustees a power to create charges on the trust assets to secure such debts, or, more boldly, that statute should itself confer such a power on all trustees.

(ix) *Power to partition*

Trustees of co-owned land have power, with the consent of the beneficiaries, to partition it, and may apply to the court for an order to partition co-owned chattels.

(x) Power to appoint new trustees

This power is vested in surviving trustees if there is no express provision conferring it on another. It allows trustees to keep some control over the changing character of a long-lasting settlement.

(b) Statutory administrative powers: Commonwealth and USA

If a settlor in England and Wales wishes to confer additional powers on trustees, he may do so. Other jurisdictions have already included a core sample of them, principally the following:

(xi) To maintain and repair trust property

(xii) To carry on a business

(xiii) To exchange trust property

(xiv) To borrow money

(xv) To provide residential accommodation for the beneficiaries

(c) Dispositive powers

In addition to their administrative powers, trustees also have powers which affect beneficial interests. These dispositive powers throw further light on the nature of trusteeship. Settlors appear of late to have cast trustees more and more in the role of their *alter ego*, their other self. Powers of appointment have long been given to trustees and amount to a significant delegation of dispositive power by the settlor. Powers given to trustees to declare new trusts, if upheld, will have taken the process one stage further, though of course the living settlor may in the real world still be doing the manipulating, particularly if trustees are professional people who rely on the settlor for business of other sorts. A letter from a settlor which says 'I would like you to do so and so . . .' will have no legal force, but it may be determinative of behaviour.

WHEN IS A TRUST NOT A TRUST?

It is a real question, how far settlors can by express powers modify the institutional trust. There must come a point at which the modification is so extensive that a court will have to say that the arrangement is contract, not trust, or else strike out the power as inconsistent. Powers given by will to trustees to declare trusts approach one boundary. Powers to trustees to profit from the trust, to delegate their discretions, to act without reasonable care, appear startling even when they appear singly. But they each derogate from the fundamental duties, and cumulatively they may amount to a recharacterisation of the arrangement by reducing beneficiary protection to an illusion. Whether these exclusion clauses will be subject to legislation which attacks unfair contract terms is a moot point. When settlors add, to this array, powers to themselves, not only to revoke the trust, but to interfere in its investment policy, for example, the difficulty is aggravated. When is a trust not a trust?

STATUTORY DISPOSITIVE POWERS

The dispositive powers of trustees conferred by statute include:

(i) Power of maintenance

This power is sometimes given expressly, but is statutorily granted to all trustees. It allows trustees to distribute income for the maintenance, education or benefit of an infant beneficiary, whether his interest is vested or contingent, and on majority imposes a duty to pay the whole income to an adult contingent beneficiary until his interest becomes vested, or he dies or his interest fails. The power only applies where no holder of a prior interest exists, for example a life tenant, to whom all the income will be due, but subject to that, it should be noted that income may, under this power, be appropriated to the benefit of someone who never attains a vested interest.

(ii) Power of advancement

Under this power, up to one half of the capital sum to which a contingent beneficiary may become entitled may be applied for his advancement or benefit, again even though he may never acquire a vested interest, though if he does acquire a vested interest, he will be required to account for whatever he has received.

(iii) Power to make valuations

This power has the appearance of being merely administrative, but it goes beyond mere administration. Trustees may fix the value of any trust property, and any valuation they make in good faith will bind all persons interested under the trust. These valuations will affect beneficial entitlement and the power is put in this list to emphasise this aspect. The powers of compromise could just as well be grouped here. The line between disposition and administration is not entirely clear-cut.

4. IMMUNITIES

Although, under the pristine trust, trustees are not to acquire a benefit, they need not, in the due execution of the trust, sustain a loss. Even trustees who are in breach may not have to bear the full consequences.

(i) As against the trust assets, the trustee is entitled to be reimbursed for costs incurred in the due administration of the trust, and has a lien over them for protection. In some cases he even has a personal remedy against the beneficiary, which he can use if the trust assets are inadequate.

(ii) In case of breach of trust, Equity's starting point was that all trustees who were in breach were jointly and severally liable to the beneficiaries for the loss. But though each trustee is theoretically liable to pay the whole and then have himself to seek equal contribution from his co-trustees, statute has now given the court power to order unequal contribution according to blame and even to excuse from contribution completely. This does not prevent the beneficiaries pursuing their trust property if it has been wrongfully alienated to one who cannot make the *Pilcher v. Rawlins* defence, though such a pursuit will reduce the loss to them and thus their claim against the trustees. There is even a view abroad that if beneficiaries cannot trace their trust property into the hands of innocent third party transferees – because, for example, it has been spent and the proceeds consumed – they may, after they have bankrupted the trustees, proceed against the pockets of those transferees. This morally bankrupt notion has a firm basis in the law of administration of deceased estates, but there is happily neither authority nor principle which makes it clearly applicable to the law of trusts generally. And a trustee who overpays a beneficiary can deduct the overpayment from other payments which the beneficiary is entitled to receive.

5. LIABILITIES

Trustees are personally liable to account for their breaches of trust, and beneficiaries may claim any property which is acquired by that breach. A more difficult question is how far trustees can be liable for breaches committed by others.

(a) The acts of agents

As we saw above, it is clear from the wording of the statute permitting delegation that a trustee will not be vicariously liable for the acts of any agent appointed in good faith. The statute does not, however, relieve the trustee of any duty which the law might impose to choose the agent responsibly and to supervise him diligently: this would be a primary liability of the trustee. In the puzzlingly worded section 30 of the Trustee Act, however, in what is described by its heading as an 'implied indemnity', a trustee is immunised against losses caused by persons like bankers with whom trust money is deposited, or for the insufficiency or deficiency of securities, unless that loss happens through his own 'wilful default'. Plainly, for some reason here, in these limited circumstances, trustees are to be excused the operation of the normal rules, and wilful default must accordingly be some lower standard than would normally apply, and something like recklessness seems the most appropriate test. Quite why only these limited situations are singled out, and why, for example, trustees who employ agents to do other acts like running businesses (where authorised) are exempted from this exemption, appears to be explicable only on the grounds that this clause, which was formerly regularly inserted into settlements, dates from a time when these acts of delegation were the principal ones permitted, and the notion was not updated in 1925. The section has been restrictively construed, but it has to be said that it would be capable of very wide construction: the deficiency of securities could be an independent head of indemnity, as could the phrase exempting trustees from liability 'for any other loss'; but such a construction would be greatly out of tune with the present mood of the judges.

(b) The acts of other trustees

There is said to be no group liability of trustees: they are only responsible for their own acts. They are also said, somewhat inconsistently, to be bound to act unanimously, in which case, of course, everything done must have been done by all trustees. It is certainly true that if they seek to use a power to avoid the operation of a duty, they must, unless they are charitable trustees, act unanimously. But a single trustee may well get in trust property on behalf of the rest, and in doing so he may well commit a breach. The fiduciary duties of trustees are, however, capable of such a wide interpretation, requiring such wide-ranging scrutiny, that it will be rare for one trustee not to have some responsibility for the acts of his colleagues. Mere inactivity is no defence to an action for breach of trust, and 'sleeping trustees' are not a category known to the law. Section 30 is now also believed to be the statutory provision which excuses him from group liability. Even if he acts by signing a receipt for the sake of conformity, he is not thereby automatically liable if the funds disappear, but, more generally, he is answerable and accountable only for his own acts, receipts, neglects, or defaults, and not for those of any other trustee, unless the loss happens through his own wilful default.

6. RIGHTS AND POWERS OF BENEFICIARIES

Apart from their merely passive role as recipients of the trust benefits, beneficiaries may play a more active role. They may bring actions to enforce any of the trust duties. The settlor may not do this. But they may not interfere with the lawful exercise of any of a trustee's powers. The powers are given to the trustees alone, and apart from the rare case of statutory intervention (land held in co-ownership under a statutory trust for sale), trustees have no obligation to listen to the wishes of the beneficiaries.

But beneficiaries may, under the rule in *Saunders v. Vautier* (1841), if they are all agreed, put an end to the trust by directing the trustees to transfer the property to them or to their direction. This will apply even inside a continuing trust, where persons entitled to income may direct the income to be applied elsewhere. This power of beneficiaries might once have been explicable on the grounds that they were in Equity owners of the property. There has recently been in Canada a resurgence of an intensely seigniorial idea, more current in medieval England and the modern USA, that the wishes of the settlor should prevail over those of the beneficiaries, and favouring abolition of the rule, thereby allowing the settlor to retain at once the benefits of contract and trust under the one device. Recent developments in the law of discretionary trusts have had two impacts on the simple *Saunders v. Vautier* rule. In the first place, relaxed rules for certainty of objects may make it impossible to gather together all the beneficiaries of such a trust, because no one may have a list of them. On the other hand, it seems clear that beneficiaries of such a trust do not have a proprietary interest in the assets, and the rule cannot therefore be an exercise of property rights. Beneficiaries of such a trust must therefore now be exercising something in the nature of a joint general power of appointment.

If the trustees and beneficiaries are in agreement, however, they may vary the trusts without terminating them and this may have fiscal advantages. No one has yet suggested that because this benefit will be lost if they do not consent, trustees must cooperate in any such scheme put forward by their beneficiaries. Agreements by beneficiaries to pay trustees are a variant of this general power. And of course if all beneficiaries decide not to pursue a breach of trust there is no one else with standing to say otherwise.

7. POWERS OF THE COURT

The court forms part of our pentad because it exercises a parental jurisdiction over trusts which is different in kind from the powers over contracts which commercial courts have exercised.

To begin with, it may itself administer a trust, and if it does the trustees may only act with the court's consent. And even if it does not take over the whole operation, the court will interfere, at the behest of beneficiaries, to the extent of questioning, and if necessary overruling, a trustee's exercise of his powers, though this is rare. More often the judges have restricted themselves to offering advice to trustees who seek it. Attempts by the settlor to cut out the court's jurisdiction by provision in the settlement giving trustees exclusive jurisdiction over the trust have met with mixed success. Generally speaking, the chances of such an exclusion clause being accepted are increased if the settlor chooses a restricted area of exclusion, if the excluded matter is primarily one of fact, if it is one the trustees (or other arbiter chosen) have some appropriate qualification for answering and, perhaps, if the settlor is tactful about it.

Courts also have a function in authorising departures from the terms of the trust. There is a limited inherent jurisdiction to vary the administrative provisions of the trust to meet emergencies; to approve, on behalf of those who cannot give consent, compromises of disputes between beneficiaries affecting beneficial interests; and to make provision for the maintenance of a minor. These powers have been mirrored and extended by statute: the Trustee Act 1925, sections 57, 53 and the Variation of Trusts Act 1958 respectively.

Finally, as we have seen, trustees who believe that they have, or may have, committed a breach of trust may apply to the court for absolution if they have acted honestly and reasonably. This is another way in which the courts may in effect make a one-off variation in the terms of a trust. This power is sometimes cited in defence of the more rigorous aspects of trustee law, such as the objective standard of care. It should be said that such an approach is at best ingenuous, at worst cynical. The horrors of litigation for non-lawyers should never be underestimated, to say nothing of the cost. We should formulate our ground rules as we would like them to be applied and not set up a draconian edifice from which we then, in court, exempt the deserving.

B. RESULTING, IMPLIED AND CONSTRUCTIVE TRUSTS

9

The Origin of the Language

Sections 51–55 and 136 of the Law of Property Act 1925 contain the formalities rules for the making of dispositions amongst the living. Section 53 imposes writing requirements on the valid creation and disposition of equitable interests. Section 53 (2) reads:

> This section does not affect the creation or operation of resulting, implied or constructive trusts.

So whatever they are, these three are exempt from the formalities rules of that section, and there are no other formalities provisions elsewhere mentioning them. (Section 40 of the statute governs contracts for interests in land, and requires writing; but contracts for resulting, implied or constructive trusts is a topic not much discussed, for reasons which will appear.)

Section 53(2) is itself a direct descendant of section 8 of the Statute of Frauds 1677. This provision exempted from its own formalities provisions any conveyance by which a trust might

> arise or result by the implication or construction of law or be transformed or extinguished by any act or operation of law.

With a lawyer's instinct to turn nouns into adjectives, we might say the statute has a notion of 'implied' or 'constructive' trusts, which might 'arise or result'.

One year earlier, Lord Nottingham had classified trusts into express or implied. *Express* trusts were declared either by 'direct and manifest proof' (words or writing), or by 'violent and necessary presumption', when the court, upon consideration of all circumstances, presumes that there was a declaration: and this last variety of express trusts, created by the court, he called 'presumptive trusts'. *Implied* trusts, on the other hand, were not created by the court, but were 'raised or created by act or construction of law'

146

(disembodied Equity again). In 1677, then, we might think, express trusts, including presumed trusts, would be caught by the formalities provisions of the new legislation. This was not to be. Trusts which 'resulted' (which were to include Lord Nottingham's 'presumed trusts' and were to be called 'resulting' trusts) were also taken out of the operation of the Act; and Lord Nottingham's implied trusts were treated alongside a separate species of constructive trusts. It should come as no surprise, therefore, to learn that from that day to this, no one has been able both to make sense of this group and impose their analysis on the rest of us. The 1925 Act's fourfold division (express, resulting, implied, constructive) was no more than a recognition of the current state of the terminology. (It also added a fifth, that of statutory trusts, set up independently of this precedent-created classification.)

THE DISAPPEARANCE OF IMPLIED TRUSTS

For a time, implied trusts included cases where a testator directed his lands to be sold for the payment of his debts and where a vendor was deemed to hold land after contract and before conveyance on trust for his purchaser. The first of these has been superseded by statutory reforms and the latter usually now reclassified, less helpfully, with constructive trusts. Implied trusts, as an independent set, appear now virtually to have disappeared. Resulting and constructive trusts only have to be identified for the purposes of section 53(2) and there is no pragmatic reason for distinguishing between them. It should be noted that if a disposition is testamentary, there is no need to identify them at all, since the Wills Act 1837 does not make an exception for such trusts. There might be thought to be some virtue in attempting to analyse the two sets in an attempt to see what informing principles drive them on, but the reality is that they represent a waste-bin category with a range of policy and principle inputs, and the division in the following account into two discrete categories is largely illusory.

10

Resulting Trusts

The first difficulty confronting a student of this group is one of language. The word 'resulting' today usually means 'being the outcome of concurring causes'. This looks very similar to 'arise or result' in the Statute of Frauds. But there is another meaning, which today seems very affected, and which comes from the overintimate connection with Latin which characterized seventeenth- and eighteenth-century English, namely to 'spring back'; resulting trusts are said to occur where a beneficial interest springs back to a grantor. This is the meaning most favoured by modern writers as it allows them to keep this category distinct from that of constructive trusts. But it is simply not the case, in any intelligible sense, that all these trusts involve the springing back of a beneficial interest. It may be the case that property goes back to someone, but the interest will in most cases never have left him. There is a similar verbal infelicity at common law with the usage of 'reversion' – that part of a grantor's interest which he has not disposed of. The land may 'revert' – the etymology of 'turn back' – but the interest has never moved. Both these are cases of conceptual thinking about interests outgrowing primitive language forms which concentrate on the movement of tangible assets. The misleading impression is greater in Equity, where beneficial enjoyment in some of these cases has never for an instant left the beneficiary of the resulting trust. A number of disparate heads are usually collected together here.

1. VOLUNTARY CONVEYANCE

Before 1925, if a grant of property was made without value passing from the grantee, it appears to have been the law that Equity would presume, unless a contrary intention of the grantor was shown, that the grantee was intended to hold the property on trust for the grantor. A similar result followed if one person voluntarily (using the artificial sense of that word, meaning 'without receiving value in return') conveyed his own property into the joint names of himself and another. So if there was a conveyance, and no other evidence of intent, the inevitable consequence was that the grantee held on resulting trust for the grantor, and had done so from the moment of the grant: no springing back of any trust interest – it was just as if A had conveyed a bare legal estate to B as trustee on trust for A himself. There is a further rather curious sub-rule: where a presumption of resulting trust was rebutted by evidence in a situation of conveyance into joint names, and it appeared that the grantor, now dead, had kept the whole income during his life, his estate was not called to account for a half share of it. The presumption as a whole is indeed curious on any view and operates in Equity as a presumption against generosity.

The origins of this bizarre rule are not easy to find. If we can believe Lord Chancellor Bacon (in his *Reading on the Statute of Uses*) it owes its origin to a paranoid intervention in the land law by sixteenth-century Chancellors. Bacon judged (that is, guessed) that *uses* of land had become very common, but while conveyances of legal estates were well publicised, equitable arrangements were secret. So where a grantee claimed to hold beneficially, the Chancellors 'thought it more convenient' to put the burden of proof on the grantee to show that he was intended to take beneficially (showing value given would be one way of doing this), rather than have the grantor prove that there was intended to be a use for himself. To avoid this resulting use, settlors came to make conveyances 'unto and to the use of' their grantees. When trusts replaced uses, the doctrine of resulting uses was transferred to the new law of trusts, and in the enthusiasm for inventing doctrine to impress and confuse ordinary folk, somehow the rule appears to have spread across to grants of chattels, though there is not a wealth of authority for this extension.

The legislators of 1925 appear to have decided to do away with this presumption, and their way of doing so may reflect their lack of confidence in the status which the doctrine enjoyed at that time. Section 60(3) of the Law of Property Act 1925 provided that such a trust shall not be 'implied merely by reason that the property is not expressed to be conveyed for the use or benefit of the grantee', which is no more than saying it will not be implied merely because it has not been rebutted. In accordance with a general desire to keep this branch of the law alive, it seems to be the generally accepted view that 'property', which the statute says includes personal property, unless the context otherwise 'requires', in this subsection means only real property.

THE CONTRA-PRESUMPTION OF ADVANCEMENT
The presumption of resulting trust is slightly mitigated in its barbarity by a rule known as the presumption of advancement, which provides that if a man makes a voluntary transfer to his wife, or child born within a marriage, or if anyone makes such a transfer to a person to whom they stand *in loco parentis*, in the place of a parent, there is a presumption that such a transfer is to take effect as a gift. But this doctrine is overlaid, in England at least, with mystical overtones. It only applies where an 'equitable obligation' exists to provide for the transferee. Transfers by mothers to their children or by 'illegitimate or non-marital' fathers to theirs, will invoke the presumption of resulting trust. So if a mother quite secretly puts property in the name of her child and dies, the presumption will operate to make the child trustee for the mother's estate.

In this case it is sometimes said that the presumption of resulting trust is rebutted by the presumption of advancement. But since the presumption of advancement may itself be rebutted (not an easy thing to do in the case of a child), and since presuming advancement only after presuming resulting trust presupposes an overly selective view of the initial facts ('now he tells me, she's the grantor's wife'), it seems preferable at a technical level to say that we should first of all see who the grantee is, apply the appropriate presumption, and then see if there is evidence to rebut it.

IRREBUTTABLE PRESUMPTIONS?
The presumption has recently been the cause of some slight judicial embarrassment at the highest level in the UK (though there seems to be more enthusiasm in Canada and Australia). It has manifested itself in two somewhat inconsistent observations. The first is that the presumption of resulting trust and that of advancement between husband and wife are now much weaker than they used to be because of changed social conditions (after all, 1987 is not 1587, is it?). But it

is also said, in an attempt to reduce its influence still further, that the presumption is only applied if no evidence of intention can be found. If this is truly meant, there can be no true presumption, since it will be irrebuttable, and we have a proposition of law to deal with cases where we have no evidence of intention. Why we still ignore the fact of transfer if we are not sure what our transferor intended is not explained. This refusal to let property lie where it falls has, however, been much more troublesome in the next category.

2. PURCHASE IN THE NAME OF ANOTHER

Another presumption rule, applying equally to chattels and land, was declared in a 'leading case' of 1788. In *Dyer v. Dyer*, Eyre CB declared that 'the trust of a legal estate . . . whether taken in the names of the purchasers and others jointly, or in the names of others without that of the purchaser; whether in one name or several; whether jointly or [successively], results to the man who advances the purchase money . . . [I]t goes on a strict analogy to the rule of common law, that where a feoffment [meaning 'grant'] is made without consideration, the use results to the feoffor.' The 'rule of common law' is the rule which produces the 'voluntary conveyance resulting trust' just discussed; 'common law' meaning case law, outside statute (in this case almost certainly contrasting this provenance with one from the Statute of Uses 1536). There is thus one informing idea supporting this head and the last.

Surprisingly, however, nothing in the 1925 legislation undermines the presumption in these cases, and it has been a cause of much litigation in the last few decades in cases concerning the acquisition of residential property by people living together in some form of close relationship. Nor has there been any serious re-evaluation of the rule in modern circumstances: the most that seems to have happened is that the idea of purchase contributions has been extended to take account of the complexity of acquisition by instalment mortgage. Perhaps the explanation lies in the observation of Deane J in the High Court of Australia in the 1985 case of *Calverly v. Green* when he described the presumptions as too well entrenched as landmarks in the law of property to be simply discarded by judicial decision, needing legislative reform if people's dispositions were to mean what they said. The presumption is again subject to the operation of the rules on advancement mentioned above, also much weakened by recent decisions.

RESULTING TRUSTS, CONSTRUCTIVE TRUSTS AND ESTOPPEL

We cannot pretend, in the present state of the authorities, to see with ease how the courts are fitting this part of the law into that of two other areas which hem it in. The first is that of constructive trust (when perceived as a distinct entity) and the second is that of proprietary estoppel. All three areas have seen rapid movement and their relationship to each other has therefore constantly changed. It might not be too bold, however, to say that there appear to be three basic cases.

First where A purchases property in her own name but in which she intends that her spouse or spouse-equivalent, B, shall have an equitable interest. This is an express trust and should, by section 53 of the Law of Property Act 1925, be in writing. Second, A purchases property which she directs her vendor to convey into the sole name of B. Here the presumption will operate. The interest will not 'spring back' to A: she will have acquired an equitable interest in the property from the moment of contract, and even without a contract, no measurable moment exists in which an equitable interest is vested in B. The effect of a resulting trust is that B will have received the property as trustee for A. Similarly, if A purchases and directs her vendor to convey into the joint names of herself and B, B will hold his share in the property on resulting trust for A. The presumption will also operate to divide the beneficial interest if A and B jointly purchase the property and direct it to be conveyed into the name of one of them. That one will hold the property on resulting trust in shares which reflect the contribution to the purchase price. Third, A purchases property in her own name but agrees with B that B shall have an equitable interest in the property and B acts to his detriment on the basis of that common agreement. This produces an interest for B, under a constructive trust (*Grant v. Edwards*, 1986). The difference between the second and third situations appears to be that in the second, the equitable interest follows the purchase money if there is no contrary evidence, while in the third the interest is created by proof of an intention along with acts of detriment. This third case also bears striking similarities to the equitable doctrine of proprietary estoppel. In this latter case, however, there does not need to be agreement, merely a representation by one party to another, which the latter acts upon; though it is clear in both cases that the court does not limit itself to giving effect to the representation or agreement, but will do what is just and equitable in the circumstances.

All that the courts now need do is find some magic wand which will readily distinguish contributions to the purchase price from detrimental acts not forming part of the consideration for the purchase of the house, particularly where payment is to be by instalments, and agreements from representations, and this simple little scheme will cause no more problems. The present complexities belong in the books on real property, where the doctrine will be seen to be a trap for third parties, causing endless difficulties in the law of registration; or in books on family law, where it will be seen that by statute, on the termination of marriage, the court has wide discretion to vary the property rights of the spouses, whatever they are.

So does the remote and irrelevant past mould the lives of ordinary folk. It has to be asked whether the man on the Clapham omnibus would not expect a starting point where documents meant what they said.

3. FAILURE TO EXHAUST THE BENEFICIAL INTEREST

This manifestation of the resulting trust seems to be an application of ordinary principles of property law. If I give land to trustees on trust for A for life, plainly I keep the rest of the interest which endures after A's death. Nothing springs back to me; what I have, never left me. This is what the common lawyers called a reversion. If I give land to trustees on trust for A for life, remainder to the first child to be born to A after the making of the gift, and A has no such child, the land will be held on trust for me after A's death. This is called a resulting trust, though again it does not spring back in any theoretical sense. This rule does not depend on a presumption of intention, but on a simple process of proprietary arithmetic; what I once had and have not granted away, I keep. It will not matter that I intended to grant it away or that I wished I had; if I have not effectively alienated, I keep what I had. My intention is relevant only as a component in interpreting what I have in fact done. This simple truth received judicial recognition by Megarry J in *Re Vandervell's Trusts No. 2* (1974).

It may thus be crucial to the success or failure of an operation whether the court characterizes a transaction as a voluntary conveyance, with a presumption of a resulting trust, which may be rebutted by evidence of contrary intention; or as a failure to exhaust the beneficial interest, where the deed, once done, cannot be undone by any amount of talk. A gift to trustees, without more said, has been construed equally plausibly as a voluntary conveyance to the trustees or as a gift on trust without trusts declared, i.e. as a failure to exhaust (*Vandervell v. IRC*, 1967). The first view allows a settlor to be rid of property he does not want, by persuading the court that that was his intention; the second leaves it inexorably with him. There are no abstract rules which say how in all cases the court must characterize the gift and so a judge may still on occasion be able to reach the result he wants by choosing how to describe the transaction.

FAILURE TO EXHAUST AND PURPOSE TRUSTS

The problem becomes more difficult in the case of trusts which are established for purposes, where the purposes fail, either initially or subsequently. This account presumes that Goff J in *Re Denley* (1969) succeeded in establishing the validity of trusts for purposes which directly or indirectly benefit individuals. Trusts for abstract purposes (unless they are in the 'anomalous' class) are presently void, at least if they are so characterized by the court. If a purpose trust's purpose fails, what happens to the property which was subjected to it? In the case where the failure is initial, it seems that the beneficial interest remains with the settlor. In the case of subsequent failure, at present where the trust is for a purpose which benefits individuals within a family, the courts have tended to say that the gift becomes absolute, but where the trust is for strangers they have given the property back to the donors on a resulting trust. This may, however, simply be another case where there are two possible constructions of the gift. If a gift has a 'superadded direction' this may be treated in the family cases as merely the motive for the gift and may in effect be ignored by the donee – not a *Denley* purpose trust at all. In such a case the failure of the purpose expressed in the superadded direction is irrelevant. But if the direction is integrated into the gift itself, the answer must be different and this may be how the cases are to be reconciled.

If we return to the example of a trust to educate children, given as an example of a valid purpose trust earlier in the book, and where our settlor makes it crystal clear that education is not the motive, but the fundamental and sole purpose of the gift, there are two possible failure scenarios. The first is that the education is successfully completed and there is a balance. The second is where the purpose is frustrated, either by the act of the child or the act of a third party (the child's university is closed down, say). In both cases, if the purpose is integrated into the gift, if it is part of the disposition, the balance should go on resulting trust to the estate (a real springing back?) or to residuary legatees (springing sideways or forward – the transulting or prosulting trust?). In the first case, however, especially where there is no express residuary gift, we can envisage that a court might wish not to send the balance back. The different answers in the cases may reflect this diffidence, though presently under the 'superadded direction' device. If so, it may be another example of judges retaining control of the result by control of characterization of the gift.

4. CLUBS AGAIN

The law becomes more difficult, however, when the property subject to the purpose trust is held for the benefit of an unincorporated association, a club, and the club fails or is deliberately dissolved. It is still not clear whether, when judges tell us how clubs hold their property, they are explaining how it could be held, embarking on some abstract exercise to save themselves the substantial embarrassment of having to hold that English law has been unable to come to terms with this simple social construct, or whether they are genuinely seeking to discover what the parties perceived themselves to be doing. If we do the latter, it seems there are four possible ways in which clubs could be holding property, and there is no theoretical reason why an individual club treasurer should not be holding its total assets on all four different bases.

STRUCTURES OF CLUB PROPERTY

First, the treasurer may be holding property on trust for the members absolutely and beneficially. This will be rare. Secondly, he may hold money on a mandate, though it seems as though courts will require very clear evidence to find this in the case of a simple club. Thirdly, he may hold it on trust for the members beneficially, but subject to their contractual duties to other members of the club, as expressed in its actual or constructive rules. Lastly, if the club promotes purposes which benefit individuals, either its own members or outsiders, it may be held on trust for the purposes of the club in general, or some particular part of them. Clubs which promote 'non-anomalous' abstract purposes will not be able to take property under this last head, unless the purposes are charitable, in which case they will be valid under the law of charity. A gift to a club which pursues charitable purposes will usually be construed to be on trust for its purposes.

CLUB FAILURE

If the club now fails, the first group of assets will already have been held absolutely for the members, and they will take them. If the assets are held subject to a mandate, even one that has become irrevocable by mixing, the assets should go back to the mandator, to whom on one view they have always belonged, unless irrevocability entails that they go to the Crown as *bona vacantia*. If held on the property-subject-to-contract basis, the members at the instant of dissolution should take those shares which they held at that instant, the dissolved contractual duties no longer keeping them from their property; but it has to be said that on occasion the Crown has succeeded in making a steal and taking as *bona vacantia*, though these cases have had unusual characteristics. None of these is resulting trust. But if the property was held on purpose trusts, it should go back to the transferor (certainly in the case of a donor; less evidently where he has received value, to avoid him getting value twice, and where *bona vacantia* may again be appropriate), and some cases have so held. It has also been held that the *bona vacantia* solution is to apply even to gifts made via collecting boxes, on the basis of an irrebuttably presumed intention that people who give in collecting boxes do not want to see their money back whatever happens – a sensible solution, but another example of attributing a desirable result to a constructive intention of parties.

ALLEGED DOCTRINAL VULNERABILITY

These last cases, involving the resulting trust solution, at least for assets which have arisen as the result of members' subscriptions, have nevertheless come in for some judicial criticism on theoretical grounds, and that from quarters which advocate the property-subject-to-contract theory, surely one of the most theoretically defective of all modern equitable constructs. The criticism is that different judges have applied the resulting trust in different ways and in ways which are inconsistent with principle. For example, in the *Printers' Protection* case (1899), where accounts had been poorly kept and where the club had a long history, an order was made distributing among present members only at the date of dissolution. This, it is now said, has two unprincipled characteristics. First, it cuts out people who on a proprietary view of a resulting trust are entitled – resulting trusts must send property back to all contributors alike. If they are dead, their estates can take the property. Secondly, and as a corollary, this method must mean that some members are taking out property which others put in. Likewise, a judge who on a resulting trust solution imposes hotchpot limitations, that is who insists that anyone taking on distribution must first put back in what he took out, is also violating property principles (*Re Hobourn Aero*, 1946). This reasoning has led to an expression of opinion favouring the property-subject-to-contract solution as analytically superior (*Golcar Sunday School* case, 1973).

A DEFENCE OF THE OLD LAW AGAINST THE NEW

These criticisms are unwelcome for two reasons. First, it may be most unjust to apply equal division on dissolution. It is true, in the case of membership subscriptions, that the longer one has been a member, the longer one has had the benefits of the club, and so division according to length of service will not, at first sight, be appropriate. But members' subscriptions may not just go towards paying for the upkeep of facilities; they may go towards their acquisition, and a member may only intend this latter part of his contribution to be a gift to his fellow members on the understanding that the club continues. A member who retires and the next day sees his one-time colleagues selling off the club assets as part of a commercial development and pocketing the proceeds may justly feel two-timed. The 'equal division amongst survivors' doctrine has not yet shown itself capable of inventing rules to meet this situation: formulating the necessary implied term will need some ingenuity. The resulting trust cases have shown flexibility according to circumstance.

But perhaps the more important criticism is the second. One of the themes of this book is that a great variety of creatures are presently caged under the heading 'trust'. Just because they are all kept together by the same keepers does not mean they all have the same characteristics. The criticisms of the resulting trust of the type we are now considering seem based on an idea of a trust which is fundamentally that of the institutional express private trust. If resulting trusts do not do backwards what express private trusts do forwards, they cannot, it seems to be said, be called trusts, and more seriously, since there is no other category, they cannot exist. This is the kind of thinking which inspired the draftsman of the Perpetuities and Accumulations Act 1964 to provide, in section 12, that a 'possibility of a resulting trust' in circumstances which might comprehend the present, should be subject to the rule against perpetuities: if it could not be done as an express private trust, it cannot be done.

This entirely overlooks one possibility, that of the remedial resulting trust. The idea of a remedial trust is one which has been much canvassed in the area of constructive trusts. Briefly, in this context the implications of calling a trust remedial are that it is not bound by the institutional characteristics of the paradigm proprietary trust. We do not mean that it is remedial in the sense that specific performance, injunction or damages are remedies. We mean that it is moulded to remedy a grievance which other concepts of the law have been unable to solve, because it is not strictly tied to the structure of those concepts. The judge's order that such and such be done will be enforced by the remedies in the narrow sense, like injunction. The old resulting trust cases on club dissolution are treating the resulting trust as a remedy in this wider sense, though, it has to be said, in an instinctive, unselfconscious way and without articulation. It is as sensible and just to exclude the long dead and untraceable, and donors by collecting box, as it is to insist, where the club is short-lived, and substantial distributions have been made, to distribute amongst all, subject to hotchpot. The constitutional and analytical advantage of this approach is that judicial discretion is exposed for what it is, instead of hiding behind metaphysical exercises constructing mechanisms quite unthought-of by the parties, and indeed maybe quite horrifying to them (the idea that members of an anti-vivisection society are free to spend the money on themselves). The discretion, being judicial, would be exercised in a reasoned way and would build up guidelines to assist parties who wished to agree without resort to court. To those who object to judicial discretion in property law, it should be said that the objection to it is usually based on the impossibility of planning, because of the uncertainty it produces. By the very nature of the problem here, we are dealing with situations which were not planned, and so the objection loses much of its force. Nor is it the case that the approach identified would prejudice third parties. It is of the essence of the remedial resulting trust that the judge is able to take circumstance into account in making allocations, and the existence of third party dependence would be a factor in the just outcome.

5. INROADS ON RESULTING TRUSTS: THE *CY-PRÈS* DOCTRINE FOR CHARITY

If an identified purpose of a gift is charitable, it may be lifted out of the ambit of these failure rules and become, subject to the quaintly named *cy-près* doctrine. It has to be said, first, that charitable-purpose trusts do not fail as easily as private ones. Gifts to defunct charitable unincorporated associations will normally be construed as gifts to their purposes, and if those purposes remain possible, there is no failure. Likewise, a defunct charitable trust may be discovered still alive, but buried inside an amalgamation. However, if a gift for a charitable trust, including a gift to a defunct charitable corporation, does suffer initial failure, the property goes on a resulting trust, unless the donor had some overwhelming or paramount intent to give to charity, and not just to the specific charity named. If there is such a paramount intent, the court will make a *cy-près* scheme, applying the property to some 'very close' purpose. If, however, a charitable purpose fails after the property has once vested in a charitable purpose, then unless the donor expressly provides for some valid gift over, the gift will always be applied *cy-près*. This last rule in particular reflects the quasi-corporate perception of charity in general by the Chancery judges, reflected also in some of the rules governing its trustees, such as their power to act by majority. Indeed the detailed working out of the 'failure' cases is a good example of the point that it is out of understanding complex things that one comes to understand simple things, in this case the nature of charity. Statute has also intervened to prevent resulting trusts in all cases where property is gathered by collecting-boxes for charity, and to confer the kind of discretionary powers on judges in respect of redistribution, which they are presently spurning in the cases involving failure of non-charitable clubs.

11

Constructive Trusts

This must be the strangest collection of cases ever gathered together under one head. The subject matter ranges in time from some of the earliest heads of equitable liability to cases which lie on the very frontier of the modern jurisdiction. Some constructive trustees will have acquired their status as the result of improper conduct, others will simply have acquired property in circumstances where, under some principle of Equity, it is considered improper that it should be retained. If we include, as some modern writers do, the vendor of land after contract and the survivor of a pact made by two (or more?) people to make wills according to the terms of the pact, we introduce examples where one becomes a trustee of property of one's own, which it is improper to treat as one's own beneficially. These last two examples have been treated in the past as implied trusts where, for the sake of such little cohesion as might be got, they might better have stayed. But the vendor-purchaser trust is now firmly identified by the judges as a constructive trust, where, as we saw earlier, it can cause nice problems in the law of dispositions of equitable interests. Whether or not we classify secret trusts as constructive trusts will have a practical importance only if we decide that they are arrangements made entirely between living people, in which case they will need exemption from the formalities requirements of the Law of Property Act 1925. If they are recognized to be testamentary, and therefore a device for avoiding section 9 of the Wills Act 1838, it will not matter what we call them since that statute has no exempting provisions for constructive trusts, and secret trusts will have to stand as judicial modification of the statute, not an application of it. The important point to note at the outset, however, is that since constructive trusts are not unified by any tightly defined governing idea, there is no logical difficulty in constraining by this device the activities of people who never handled property at all, but who have made a profit by, for example, giving advice to those who do hold the property on how improperly to derive a benefit from it. Subsuming these trusts under a governing idea like restitution may restrict the range of application.

EXPRESS TRUSTEES AND CONSTRUCTIVE TRUSTS

Many of the early examples of constructive trustees are those of express trustees acquiring profits in breach of trust. Unauthorized remuneration, purchase of the trust property or its notional extension (renewing a lease) and, perhaps, secret commissions come under this head. It is natural that such persons should hold these profits on similar terms to those on which they held their original trust assets. The trust mechanism is clamped on to the new assets for the benefit of the original beneficiaries. The constructive trust in this sense is the old familiar trust, but with assets which were not transferred to the trustee by the old familiar settlor. If the assets were no longer traceable by the beneficiaries, the trustee would face a so-called personal liability; that is, he would be obliged to make monetary recompense out of his general assets. In the light of the great variety of liability under this head, and especially if we here include the man who knowingly assists in breach of trust even though he never acquires trust assets, it seems almost to be terminologically squeamish not to identify the remedy against the trustee who no longer has identifiable assets as a constructive trust. All we need note is that highly specific rules apply to it: as they do to other examples.

SOME LOGICAL EXTENSIONS – FIDUCIARIES AND ADVISERS

Outside the strict notion of trusteeship, Equity has long had a notion of the fiduciary. The underlying idea here seems to be that where one party manages property for the benefit of another, and where the common law solution is inadequate (so, for instance, the highly successful notion of a bailment at common law is left largely alone), Equity is liable to interfere and impose on him obligations similar to, but less strict than, those of a trustee. All trustees are fiduciaries, but not all fiduciaries, in this sense, are trustees. Easily recognized fiduciary relationships are company directors with their companies, partners with each other and agents with their principals. Other people will become fiduciaries if they are involved in a management-benefit split in a particular situation. Some agents in the wide sense, like professional advisers, may be caught, as will the law's earliest fiduciary, the guardian. These people will be saddled with obligations of a slightly diminished severity, and courts are more willing to listen to explanations from them than they are from trustees. This head of liability has strong analytical associations with the doctrine of undue influence where extended notions of fiduciary obligation are imposed on people who hold others in particular thrall, such as financial or medical advisers, and then receive property from them. Such persons will be obliged to demonstrate that the transfer was made free of the influence of the relationship. Advisers of fiduciaries will also in appropriate circumstances be drawn into the net if they have assisted in the breach of a fiduciary duty. This branch of constructive trusts, along with the next, has seen some of the more dramatic recent developments. Most of these take place outside the simple context of the domestic trust and are part of a wider picture of the Chancery judges moving increasingly into the world of commerce, a development already noted with the express trust. These new moves centre around transactions by the fiduciary with a third party, in breach of his fiduciary duty, most notably company directors engaging in ventures which their companies have fought shy of, and also around the use by fiduciaries of confidential information for their own profit. This frontier reaches the very limit of the jurisdiction when confidential information acquired by non-fiduciary business associates in the course of negotiations is similarly treated. Treating confidential information as property will not be an easier way of solving these problems, due to the seemingly inherent difficulty of defining it.

NON-FIDUCIARY STRANGERS
Those who receive property subject to a fiduciary obligation, in breach of that obligation, will also be caught by this device. Intermeddlers with trust property will find themselves treated as trustees, as will recipients of trust property with notice that it is transferred in breach of trust. This will even include third parties such as banks who receive the property only as conduits. There has been much debate in this area about the nature of notice. Judicial opinion is divided on whether negligent failure to see is enough; knowledge of circumstances which would put an honest and reasonable man on

enquiry. Academic opinion, for no obvious reason, is generally hostile to negligence liability in this area, preferring to allow banks and others to mount defences based on the proposition that their branch managers need not be honest and reasonable men. If there are no theoretical objections to making express trustees liable for negligence, the only objection to making negligent persons into constructive trustees must be one of policy. That policy, if its effect is to make it more difficult to prevent the victims of company fraud from receiving recompense, has had too long a run. Finally, whether or not the innocent volunteer recipient of trust property is called a constructive trustee seems almost a matter of taste; judicial reluctance to impose such a label seems to be based on a desire not to impose the heavy duties of trusteeship. This reluctance appears to be based on the view that constructive trustees are really just trustees like express private trustees.

INEQUITABLE CONDUCT

Equity has long intervened to prevent people from benefiting from inequitable conduct such as simple fraud or criminal activity, most notably killing off their relatives from whom they would inherit. Fraud, however, is now much extended in Equity, and includes receiving the benefit of a promise and then relying on a statutory defence when called upon to perform one's half. Indeed, the use of statutory defences of this sort especially in land registration is one of the most active fields of recent judicial adventurism in England, where the constructive trust has invaded those cells previously labelled as licences, resulting trusts and proprietary estoppel, throwing all four areas into a state of some confusion, since each is seeking to achieve substantially the same result. This is the 'justice and good conscience' approach which stands at the heart of the constructive trust when perceived as a remedy; it stands on one of the interfaces between legal and moral liability. The device is not limited, in the relief it gives, to analogy from existing institutions. If an express trustee's liability is derived from his status, this is more openly Equity's law of tort. Judges have deliberately kept open the edges of doctrine to take account of socially unacceptable behaviour, as perceived by the Bench, but the analogy from the notion of express trusteeship has, in England, tended to dominate – the institutional approach. Other jurisdictions have adopted different balances between the two approaches, the English judges taking on the whole a more cautious line, a caution recently reinforced in the Court of Appeal (see, e.g., *Grant v. Edwards*). We should remember that, as Lord Nottingham long ago pointed out in *Cook v. Fountain* (1676), there are limits to legal intervention, for otherwise 'no man need to be confessed'.

ALLEGED DOCTRINAL LIMITATIONS

It is often said that two of the principal reasons for seeking to establish the constructive trust liability are to acquire profits made by the trustee under the accounting liability, rather than sue for damages for loss (which might be less) and to impose burdens on third parties, including the securing of priority in bankruptcy (the beneficiary under a constructive trust not being seen as a mere creditor who needs to prove in the bankruptcy, but as someone whose property the bankrupt happened to be holding, and which must be subtracted before the debtors are paid). Of course, the beneficiary of an express trust has both these advantages. These advantages are not claimed for mere personal remedies against the trustee's general assets. This view, attaching extended remedies to constructive trusts, is held even by those who believe in the remedial aspect of the constructive trust. We should ask whether this is not an unidentified appendage from the old institutional modes of thought, and whether constructive trusts should attract both advantages.

There was some debate in the nineteenth century about the binding effect of constructive trusts on third party purchasers for value. Is it fair to have a doctrine of constructive notice for constructive trusts? The same might even be said about innocent volunteers. Constructive trusts may be difficult to establish, especially since their creation need not be attended by formality, and may tax the investigative powers even of an experienced judge. What should a third party transferee do when challenged with a claim from a beneficiary under such a trust? Should he simply abdicate his claim of title, or fight and risk having to pay the costs of the action? The case of *Ottaway v. Norman* (1972), discussed above, is a simple illustration. The defendant executor was relying on his own volunteer's title under the will of the secret trustee when he was faced with a writ from an alleged beneficiary of a secret trust of which he had no knowledge. After a prolonged witness action, he lost. It is hard to know how he could have been advised better on the strength of the evidence presented in court. To say that a secret trustee should be liable to account is one thing, to impose liabilities on third parties is another. In short, there is more than a trace of the old philosophy in the view that if one consequence follows, both follow. Of course if the constructive trust is a purely proprietary institutional device, they must. But there is no reason, if we see remedy first and foremost, why we should not give the profit without the third party consequences. We have seen that the constructive trust between vendor and purchaser of land is a very mixed concept. We need not get involved in disputes about whether Roman lawyers would have understood such a notion; we can return to the thought which dominates the early part of this book and talk of defeasibility. The beneficiary's right is a property right, but innocent transferees who do not take from the trustee of an express private trust could be told that it is just and equitable that the beneficiary's rights are defeated by conveyance to them, an extension of the *Pilcher v. Rawlins* (1872) idea.

12

Trustees of Resulting, Implied and Constructive Trusts

The story completes its circle with this topic. A trust, like law, is a many splendour'd thing. If all we know is that we are faced with a trust, we know only a few of its characteristics. It is most likely to involve property and will usually be replete with notions of fiduciary obligation devised by the Chancery judges. An express trustee who is in breach of trust and who is made a constructive trustee of the proceeds will be burdened with the same duties in respect of his new assets that he held with respect to those given him by his settlor. But in what sense is it right to call the unknowing infant resulting trustee, into whose name property has been secretly and voluntarily transferred, a fiduciary? Such a person can have none of the duties or powers of the express trustee and ought to have only an obligation to restore the property on demand, if still in possession of it. Even reckless disregard of property one does not know one has (the infant, grown old, but still unknowing, negligently loses the property) should not produce liability. No more should innocent transfer on. There must be other resulting trustees for whom this is also true in the purchase in the name of another context.

The innocent volunteer transferee from an express trustee in breach will hold a legal estate on trust and therefore qualifies as a trustee, but the courts' reluctance so to label him is no more than a reluctance to ascribe to him any duties beyond those of return on demand. Likewise an innocent transferee from a fully secret trustee, if he is to be bound, should not have the duties of an express trustee. The vendor of land after contract, as we saw, is a trustee who is not bound by the 'no profit from the trust' rule, and a transferor in a voluntary conveyance into joint names where the presumption of resulting trust is rebutted appears to be entitled to retain the whole of the income during his life. Trustees under the inequitable conduct head of liability of constructive trust may not know until judgment what they are supposed to be trustees of, and yet the judgment is not

167

simply forward-looking. It is hard to see how they could have been previously performing their trustee duties. There are evidently many kinds of trustee.

The fact that most, if not all, of this last section cannot be controversial is firm evidence that the remedial 'trust' already has a firm foothold in English law. 'Trust', in the common law world, tells us no more than that we are investigating a legal relationship owing its intellectual history to the English Court of Chancery. If we wish to know more, we must explore the particular usage under investigation.

Ecumenical (and Catholic) Bibliography

AUSTRALIA

Baxt, R. and Marks, B, *The Law of Trusts*, 1981
Chesterman, M., *Charities, Trusts and Social Welfare*, 1979
Cope, M., *Duress, Undue Influence and Unconscionable Bargains*, 1985
Finn, P.D., *Fiduciary Obligation*, 1977
——*Essays in Equity*, 1985
Ford, H.A.J. and Hardingham, J., *Cases on Trusts*, 1984
——and Lee, W.A., *Principles of the Law of Trusts*, 1983
——*Unincorporated Non-Profit Associations*, 1959
Fricke, G. and Strauss, O.K., *Law of Trusts in Victoria*, 1964
Grbich, Y.F.R., Munn, G.D. and Reicher, H., *Modern Trusts and Taxation*, 1978
Hardingham, J. and Baxt, R., *Discretionary Trusts*, 1984
Heydon, J.D., Gummow, W.M.C. and Austin, R.P., *Cases and Materials on Equity and Trusts*, 1982
Jacobs' Law of Trusts in Australia, ed. R.P. Meagher and W.M.C. Gummow, 1986
Jacobs' Law of Trusts in NSW, 1971
Jackson, D.C., *Principles of Property Law*, 1967
Jordan, F., *Select Legal Papers: Chapters on Equity in NSW*, 1983
Kercher, B. and Noone, M., *Remedies*, 1983
Meagher, R.P., Gummow, W.M.C. and Lehane, J.R.F., *Equity: Doctrines and Remedies*, 1984
Spry, I.C.F., *The Principles of Equitable Remedies: Injunctions, Specific Performance and Equitable Damages*, 1984
Starke, J.G., *Assignments of Choses in Action in Australia*, 1972

Law Reform Commission of Australia, *The Law Reform Digest*, Vol. I, 1910–80 at p. 652; Vol II, 1980–5 at p. 207; contains notes and summaries of 45 reports on the law of trusts from Australasian jurisdictions, as well as cross-references to related reports.

CANADA (except Quebec)

Cullity, M.C. and Forbes, R.E., *Taxation and Estate Planning*, 1978
Fridmann, G.H.L. and McCleod, J.G., *Restitution*, 1982
Klippert, G.W., *Unjust Enrichment*, 1983
Oosterhoff, A.H., *Cases and Materials on the Law of Trusts*, 1980 (new edition with E. Gillese, pending)
Raphael, L.R., *Canadian Income Taxation of Trusts*, 1982
Sharpe, R.J., *Injunctions and Specific Performance* 1983
Shepherd, J.C., *The Law of Fiduciaries*, 1981
Smith, B.G., *Introduction to the Canadian Law of Trusts*, 1979
Waters, D.W.M., *The Law of Trusts in Canada*, 1984
——*The Law of Trusts in the 80s*, 1980
——*The Constructive Trust*, 1964

The Uniform Law Conference of Canada has from time to time considered the law of trusts. See its *Proceedings: Uniform Law Section* for the years 1924–9, 1946–7, 1951, 1959–61, 1965–70 and 1985.

Alberta Institute of Law Research and Reform, *The Rule in Saunders v. Vautier*, 1972
Manitoba Law Reform Commission, *Report on Investment Provisions under the Trustee Act*, 1982
Manitoba Law Reform Commission, *Report on The Rules against Accumulations and Perpetuities*, 1982
Ontario Law Reform Commission, *Report on the Law of Trusts*, 1984

COLOMBIA

Rengifo, R., *La Fiducia: Legislacion Nacional y Derecho Comparado*, 1984

ENGLAND and WALES

Bacon, F., *Reading on the Statute of Uses*, 1600 (reprinted 1892)
Bean, D., *Injunctions*, 1984
Birks, P., *An Introduction to the Law of Restitution*, 1985
Chesterman, M., *Charities, Trusts and Social Welfare*, 1979
Day, M. and Harris, P., *Unit Trusts: the Law and Practice*, 1974
Goff, R. and Jones G., *The Law of Restitution*, 1978
Hanbury, H.G. and Maudsley, R.H. *Modern Equity*, ed. J. Martin, 1985
Harris, J.W., *Variation of Trusts*, 1975
Hayton, D.J. and Marshall, O.R., *Cases and Commentary on the Law of Trusts*, 1986

Ecumenical (And Catholic) Bibliography

Hayton, D.J., *Registered Land*, 1981

Jones, G., *A History of the Law of Charity*, 1969

Jones, G. and Goodhart, W., *Specific Performance*, 1986

Keeton, G.W., and Sheridan, L.A., *The Law of Trusts*, 1983

——*Equity*, 1976 (updated by 'booklets')

——*A Digest of the English Law of Trusts*, 1979

Keeton, G.W., *A Casebook on Equity and Trusts*, 1974

Lawson, F.H. and Rudden, B., *The Law of Property*, 1982

Lawson, F.H., (and Teff, H.), *Remedies of English Law*, 1980

Lewin on Trusts, ed. W.J. Mowbray, 1964

Maitland, F.W., *Equity* ed. J. Brunyate, 1936; and ed. A.H. Chaytor and W.J. Whittaker, 1985

Marsh, A.H., *History of the Court of Chancery and the Rise and Development of the Doctrines of Equity*, 1890 (reprinted in the USA, 1985)

Marshall, O.R., *The Assignment of Choses in Action*, 1950

Maudsley, R.H., *The Modern Law of Perpetuities*, 1979

Maudsley, R.H., and Burn, E.H., *Trusts and Trustees: Cases and Materials*, 1984

Mellows, A.R., *Taxation for Executors and Trustees*, 1981

——*Trustees' Handbook*, 1975

Milsom, S.F.C., *Historical Foundations of the Common Law*; ch. 9 1981

Morris, J.H.C. and Leach, W.B., *The Rule against Perpetuities*, 1962

Mortmain statutes, see Jones, G. (above) for references

Murphy, W.T. and Clark, L. *The Family Home*, 1983

Oakley, A.J., *Constructive Trusts*, 1987

Ockelton, M. *Trusts for Accountants*, 1987

Parker, D.B. and Mellows, A.R., *The Modern Law of Trusts*, 1983

Pettit, P.H., *Equity and the Law of Trusts*, 1984

Picarda, H., *The Law and Practice Relating to Charities*, 1977

Riddall, J.G., *The Law of Trusts*, 1982

Sheridan, L.A., *Fraud in Equity*, 1957

Sheridan, L.A. and Keeton, G.W., *The Modern Law of Charities*, 1983

Sladen, M., *Practical Trust Administration*, 1983

Snell's Principles of Equity, ed. Baker, P.V. and Langan, P.St J., 1982

Soares, P.C., *Trusts and Tax Planning*, 1979

Thomas, G.W., *Taxation of Trusts*, 1981

Tiley, J., *A Casebook of Equity and Succession*, 1968

Tudor on Charities, ed. S.G. Maurice, D.B. Parker, S. Finn and J. Warburton, 1984

Underhill: The Law relating to Trusts and Trustees; ed. D.J. Hayton, 1979

Venables, R., *Tax Planning through Trusts*, 1983

Inheritance Tax Planning Through Trusts, 1987

Vinter, E., *A Treatise on the History and Law of Fiduciary Relationship and Resulting Trusts*, 1955

Waters, D.W.M., *The Constructive Trust*, 1964
White, P., *Trusts: Maximising the Tax Advantages*, 1983

Law Reform Committee (23rd Report), *The Powers and Duties of Trustees* 1982 (Cmnd 8733)

FRANCE

Amos and Walton: Introduction to French Law, ed. F.H. Lawson, A.E. Anton and L.N. Brown, 1967
Dalloz; Encyclopaedia/Repertoire de Droit International 1969: entry 'Trust' in Vol II, by F. Aubert
Lepaulle, P., *Traite theorique et pratique des Trusts,* 1932

GERMANY (recent approximations)

Liebich, V.D. and Mathews, K., *Treuhand und Treuhander in Recht und Wirtschaft: Ein Handbuch*, 1983
Sorg, M.H., *Die Familienstiftung: Wesen, Probleme, Gestaltungsvorschlage fur die Praxis*, 1984

INDIA

Aggarwal, A.K., *Commentary on the Indian Trusts Act 1882*, 1984
Basu, N.D., *Law of Injunctions*, 1965
Diwan, P., *Tax Planning for Public and Private Trusts in the Conspectus of the Tax Laws*, 1985
Ghandi, B.M., *Equity, Trusts and Specific Relief*, 1983
Goyle, L.C., *The Law of Specific Performance*, 1984
Mukherjea, B.K., *The Hindu Law of Religious and Charitable Trusts*, 1970
Mukherjee, A.N., *The Indian Trusts Act 1882: with Model Forms of Private Family Trust Deeds*, 1983
Srinivasan, K., *Tax Treatment of Private Trusts*, 1983
Woodroffe, J.G. (and Mistra, S.C.), *The Law Relating to Injunctions*, 1964

Ecumenical (And Catholic) Bibliography

IRISH REPUBLIC

Keeton, G.W. and Sheridan, L.A., *The Comparative Law of Trusts in the Commonwealth and the Irish Republic*, 1976
Wylie, J.C.W., *Irish Land Law*, 1975
——*Casebook on Equity and Trusts in Ireland*, 1985

LIECHTENSTEIN

Biedermann, C. (trans. H.G. Crossland); *The Trust in Liechtenstein Law: a Comparison with its Prototype in the Common Law Trust*, 1984

NETHERLANDS

Dyer, V.A. and Loon, J.H.A., *Anglo-Amerikaanse Trusts in het Nederlandse Recht: Preadvisen*, 1983

NEW ZEALAND

Garrow and Kelly's Law of Trusts and Trustees, ed. N.C. Kelly, 1982
McKay, L., *Cases and Materials on Trusts*, 1980
Nevill's Trusts, Wills and Administration, ed. J.W. Brown, 1976
Spencer Bower, G. and Turner A.K., *The Law Relating to Estoppel by Representation*, 1977

Property Law and Equity Reform Committee 1985 on Trustees' Powers of Investment (and see last entry for Australia)

SCOTLAND

Walker, D.M., *Principles of Scottish Private Law*, Vol. IV, 1983
Wilson, W.A. and Duncan, A.G.M., *Trusts, Trustees and Executors*, 1974

SOUTH AFRICA

Fairburn, W.J.G., *Handbook for Trustees and Executors*, 1973
Honoré, A.M., *The South African Law of Trusts*, 1985
Shrand, D., *Trusts in South Africa*, 1976

South African Law Commission, *Project 9 Report on the Law of Trusts*, 1983

SRI LANKA

Cooray, L.J.M., *The Reception in Ceylon of the English Trust*, 1971

SWITZERLAND

Dreyer, D.A., *Le Trust en Droit Suisse*, 1981

UNITED STATES (except Louisiana)

Bogert, G.G. and G.T., *Hornbook on Trusts*, 1973
Bogert, G.G., *The Law of Trusts and Trustees*, 1965 and supplements
Chaffee and Re, *Cases and Materials on Equity*, ed. E.D. Re, 1975
Fiss, O.M., *Injunctions*, 1972
Hill, M.G., Rossen, H.M. and Sogg, W.S., *Remedies: Equity – Damages – Restitution*, 1984
McGovern, W.M., *Cases and Materials on Wills, Trusts and Future Interests*, 1982
Newman, R.A., *Equity and Law: a Comparative Study*, 1961
Nossaman, W.L. and Wyatt, J.L., *Trust Administration and Taxation*, 1957
Palmer, G.E., *Cases and Materials on Trusts and Succession*, 1983
Pound, R., Griswold, E. and Sutherland A.E. (eds.), *Perspectives on Law: Essays for Austin Wakeman Scott*, 1964
Sederbaum, A.D., *Income Taxation of Estates and Trusts*, 1985
Scott on Trusts, 1967 and supplements
Solomon, L.D., *Trust and Estates, a Basic Course: Problems, Planning and Policy*, 1984
Story's Commentaries on Equity Jurisprudence as Administered in England and America, revised by J.W. Perry, 1984
Turner, G.M., *Irrevocable Trusts*, 1985

American Law Institute, *Restatement of the Law, Second – Trusts 2d*, 1959 (the Institute also has publications on the trusts laws of individual states and issues reports from time to time via the National Conference of Commissioners on Uniform State Laws).

Individual states also have textbooks: e.g., Lowell, D.R. and Grimsley, J.G., *Florida Law of Trusts*, 1984

WORLDWIDE

de Wulf, C., *The Trust and Corresponding Institutions in the Civil Law*, 1965

Hague Conference, *Proceedings of the 15th Session of the Hague Conference on Private International Law 1984: 'Trusts – Applicable law and recognition'*, 1985. Bibliography at pp. 103–8. Final articles published in the UK as Cmnd 9494.

International Encyclopaedia of Comparative Law (under the auspices of the International Association of Legal Science), Vol. VI, *Property and Trust* (only two chapters presently written – Ch. 2. (1975) and ch. 11 (1973)

Weiser, F., *Trusts on the Continent of Europe*, 1936

Wilson, W.A., ed., *Trusts and Trust-like Devices*, 1981

Zweigert, K. and Kotz, H., An Introduction to Comparative Law, 1977, esp. pp. 274–84

A cautionary note

Exercise care in combing the bibliographical sources if you are a newcomer to the law. 'Trust' in the USA also has a meaning close to 'monopoly', and the word has a usage in public international law which is analogous to the usage in this book, but is not the same.

Cases

Numbers in bold refer to pages in the text

Statutes

Index

This index is designed to be used with the table of contents of the front of the book. Topics which are prominently advertised there are not repeated here

UNDERSTANDING TORT LAW

Carol Harlow

Tort law is the technical name for part of our system of civil liability. When people turn to the legal system for compensation for some injury which they have suffered, the rules of tort law come into play. So tort law has to deal with a wide range of situations. If a careless driver causes an accident, for example, he may be legally liable and he (or more often his insurers) will have to compensate those who have been injured. In a very different case, a householder whose neighbours disturb him by their noise or other annoying habits may want the nuisance ended. He, too, can turn to tort law. So could someone whose reputation has been damaged by a defamatory article in a newspaper. To deal with these disparate situations, tort law needs to be versatile and to keep in tune with changing social needs.

Understanding Tort Law sets out to place the modern rules of tort into their social context in order to help those who are new to the subject to follow its development. It outlines the way in which the rules are made and describes their origins in a very different society. The book also provides a simple introduction to tort law's complex and confusing rules and technical vocabulary.

UNDERSTANDING CRIMINAL LAW

C. M. V. Clarkson

The main focus of *Understanding Criminal Law* is on the general principles of criminal liability and the most important offences – homicide and the other crimes against the person, sexual offences, and the various property offences such as theft and burglary. It explains the substantive rules of criminal law within the context of the law's overall objectives, showing that the distinction between murder and manslaughter, for instance, can be properly understood only if the law's purpose is also appreciated. In doing this, the rationale of the various rules and the relationship between them is explored. This examination reveals that the criminal law is concerned with protecting certain values. The author exposes these values and subjects them to scrutiny, at times expressing preferences as to how the criminal law should develop. His book presents a straightforward and stimulating approach to understanding criminal law.

UNDERSTANDING PUBLIC LAW

Gabriele Ganz

The British constitution used to be the envy of the world; now there is hardly any element of it which has not come under attack. In exploring why this has happened, *Understanding Public Law* explains how the constitution works today.

The sovereignty of Parliament, once the hallmark of British democracy, has given rise to an elective dictatorship, the government dominating the House of Commons through the party machine. The Prime Minister's power has been growing vis-à-vis the Cabinet and Civil Service. The government increasingly uses delegated legislation, and it has greatly centralized power by imposing constraints on local government and the nationalized industries. There has been no corresponding growth in the mechanisms for accountability or public participation in decision-making. But there has been a considerable extension of police powers of arrest and detention, searching of premises and dealing with public disorder. Fundamental changes to the constitution have been recommended to remedy these defects, such as electoral reform, devolution, a Freedom of Information Act and a Bill of Rights. Without such changes the working of the constitution could be transformed if those elected to power behaved differently. A democracy is only as good as its elected representatives.

Professor Ganz's readable account of the state of public law will both clarify and provoke discussion.

UNDERSTANDING CONTRACT LAW

John Adams and Roger Brownsword

The major contention of *Understanding Contract Law* is that the legal rules regulating agreements cannot be understood without examining what lies behind those rules.

The book seeks to interpret judicial decision-making in contract cases. It portrays judges as caught in a web of tensions. They are pulled in one direction by a wish to keep faith with tradition; and in another direction by a wish to ensure acceptable outcomes to disputes, to meet commercial expectations, and to protect consumers. The outcome of any particular case will depend therefore not on the mechancial application of 'the law of contract' but on the way in which the ideological tensions which structure judges' reasoning are resolved.

This accessible yet challenging analysis of contract law provides a full introduction to the subject and puts forward new ideas.

UNDERSTANDING PROPERTY LAW

W. T. Murphy and Simon Roberts

Understanding Property Law provides the background to an area of English law which students have found particularly difficult. Originally constructed piecemeal by lawyers over the years, the law today is expressed in complex language owing much to objectives and problems from a forgotten past. The authors of this book however stand back from their subject and stress the practical character of property law, emphasizing the role of lawyers in the diverse transactions – such as sale, gift and inheritance – in which their clients become involved. The focus upon the work which lawyers do in their offices provides a necessary complement to the treatment of legislation and judicial activity found in most textbooks. In this book, English property law is revealed as a many-layered text, built up over long periods of time, and properly understood only in the light of the meanings attached to each of these layers in the past. It is a stimulating approach which makes comprehensible a subject that has often seemed obscure.